RDA Made Simple

RDA Made Simple

A Practical Guide
to the New Cataloging Rules

Amy Hart

LIBRARIES UNLIMITED

AN IMPRINT OF ABC-CLIO, LLC
Santa Barbara, California • Denver, Colorado • Oxford, England

Copyright © 2014 by Amy Hart

All rights reserved. No part of this publication may be reproduced, stored in a retrieval system, or transmitted, in any form or by any means, electronic, mechanical, photocopying, recording, or otherwise, except for the inclusion of brief quotations in a review, without prior permission in writing from the publisher.

Library of Congress Cataloging-in-Publication Data

Hart, Amy.
  RDA made simple : a practical guide to the new cataloging rules / Amy Hart.
    pages cm
  Includes bibliographical references and index.
    ISBN 978-1-61069-485-8 (paperback) — ISBN 978-1-61069-486-5 (ebook)   1. Resource description & access.   2. Descriptive cataloging—Standards.   I. Title.
  Z694.15.R47H367   2014
  025.3'2—dc23   2014023711

ISBN: 978-1-61069-485-8
EISBN: 978-1-61069-486-5

18 17 16 15 14   1 2 3 4 5

This book is also available on the World Wide Web as an eBook.
Visit www.abc-clio.com for details.

Libraries Unlimited
An Imprint of ABC-CLIO, LLC

ABC-CLIO, LLC
130 Cremona Drive, P.O. Box 1911
Santa Barbara, California 93116-1911

This book is printed on acid-free paper ∞
Manufactured in the United States of America

Contents

PART THREE: SPECIAL TOPICS AND EXAMPLES

Introduction

WHY THIS BOOK?

In this book, I seek to offer a middle path for learning RDA. The concepts behind RDA are different enough from AACR2 that catalogers should become familiar with them. In addition, there are more changes coming as the march from traditional cataloging to Web-friendly, machine-actionable, and linked data moves inexorably forward. Knowledge of RDA will be needed to understand what comes next.

At the same time, most catalogers are, perforce, practical-minded. They need to take the most efficient path to knowledge. For many, this means learning by example. Catalogers need (and want to learn from) concrete examples and straightforward instructions on how to do things.

RDA Made Simple tries to connect practical actions (here's what you do) to specific rules in RDA, and to ground both in the concepts and vocabulary that undergird them.

WHO IS IT FOR?

The book is intended for librarians who catalog at a very general level and not for specialists. Librarians who catalog a wide variety of materials and need to know "enough" about a lot of formats will benefit from it, as will those whose work is mostly copy cataloging with some original cataloging mixed in. It may also be useful for students of cataloging because it looks closely at how RDA is structured and describes an RDA-based approach to cataloging. Library directors and department managers can benefit from the information on planning and implementation. The book concentrates on the descriptive side of cataloging (the bibliographic record) and touches only tangentially on authority control practices and changes.

HOW IS IT ORGANIZED?

The book has three goals.

1. To build a bridge between AACR2 and RDA for those catalogers who know the former and need to become comfortable with the latter.
2. To offer an approach to understanding RDA's organization and text in order to develop a mental map of how cataloging is done using RDA.
3. To connect theory and rules to actual practice so that catalogers can confidently base their day-to-day decision making on the new rules and can navigate RDA to answer their questions when necessary.

The structure of the book reflects its goals.

- Part One reviews the history of RDA's development, including the U.S. Test results. Planning for implementation is discussed from a staff and organizational viewpoint, followed by a review of the major issues and decisions you will need to address. Part One then offers a review of the conceptual models behind RDA, the Functional Requirements for Bibliographic Records (FRBR) and the Functional Requirements for Authority Data (FRAD). The section concludes with a look at RDA's general characteristics and structure, offering tips for using the text and providing a concrete example of how to navigate through RDA.
- Part Two takes a close look at RDA's text. It offers an in-depth, chapter-by-chapter review of RDA's contents, identifying core elements, noting changes from AACR2, and alerting readers when the Library of Congress (LC) or the Program for Cooperative Cataloging (PCC) have issued policy statements to clarify practice. A tight focus on using RDA in a MARC environment is maintained, matching MARC coding and specific RDA rules.
- Part Three, the final section of the book, gives information on specific situations in RDA MARC cataloging and offers annotated examples of records for a variety of formats.

ACKNOWLEDGMENTS

This book would not have been possible without the help of the many librarians who have enthusiastically shared their knowledge of RDA with the library community. The amount of material made available by the Library of Congress, the Program for Cooperative Cataloging, presenters at professional meetings, and via electronic discussion lists is truly staggering. ALA's Association for Library Collections and Technical Services (ALCTS) has been offering RDA webinars for multiple years now. Online Audiovisual Catalogers (OLAC) and the Music Library Association (MLA) are just two of the several specialist organizations that have provided input for RDA's development and suggested best practices. In addition, several RDA test participants and other libraries have made their training materials available to others. To all who helped me, thank you.

That said, any errors or misunderstanding of RDA theory or practice are entirely my own. While I have done my best to be current, changes and clarifications continue fast and furious. I have presented my best understanding of RDA practice at the time of writing.

Part One

Preparing for RDA

RDA History to 2008

BACKGROUND: 1967–2004

The first *Anglo-American Cataloging Rules* (AACR) were published in 1967, with separate, and different, editions for the United States and United Kingdom. The rules were the result of work by the American Library Association (ALA) and the Library Association (UK), with input from the Canadian Library Association.

The Joint Steering Committee for the Revision of AACR (JSC) was established in 1974 and charged to review AACR and develop a single unified set of rules. Members of the JSC were the ALA, the British Library, the Canadian Library Association (represented by the Canadian Committee on Cataloguing), the Library Association, and the Library of Congress. The second *Anglo-American Cataloging Rules* were released in 1978, and known as AACR2. Revised in 1988, 1998, and 2002, these were and are the cataloging rules in place until RDA is fully adopted (JSC, "Brief History of AACR2").

2004

In 2004, the JSC began work on AACR3. By this time, the JSC group included representatives from these organizations:

- American Library Association
- Library of Congress
- British Library
- Chartered Institute of Library and Information Professionals, CILIP (UK) (formerly the Library Association)
- Canadian Committee on Cataloguing
- Australian Committee on Cataloguing

In 2012, the German National Library (Deutsche National Bibliothek) was invited to join JSC and in 2013 joined the Committee of Principals (CoP). Goals for AACR3 included the following:

- Provide the basis for improved user access to all media in an online search environment.
- Compatibility with other standards for resource description and retrieval.
- For use worldwide both by libraries and by other information agencies.
- Easier and more efficient for catalogers to use and interpret, both in a printed format and in an enhanced electronic form. (Tillett 2004)

2005

In April 2005, as a result of reaction to the draft of part I, the JSC changed the name of AACR3 to RDA: Resource Description and Access (JSC 2005). Two major reasons for the change were:

- The decision to align the new rules with FRBR (Functional Requirements for Bibliographic Records) and FRAD (Functional Requirements for Authority Data).
- A desire to include a broader community, including those working with metadata.

As a result of the JSC's redefined focus, additional stakeholders were identified and invited to participate in the development of RDA. These included:

- The **DCMI/RDA Task Group:**
  - ○ Formed in April 2007 as a result of a meeting between the JSC, the Dublin Core Metadata Initiative (DCMI), and the W3C Semantic Web Deployment Working Group, the Task Group worked on defining an RDA Element Vocabulary and registering RDA Value Vocabularies on the Web.
- **RDA/MARC Working Group:**
  - ○ The RDA/MARC Working Group was established in 2008 to develop proposals for changes to MARC21 to accommodate RDA.
- **IME ICC:**
  - ○ IFLA's "Meeting of Experts on an International Cataloging Code" developed a *Statement of International Cataloguing Principles* (2009) to update the 1961 *Paris Principles*.
- **Publishing Community and Developers of ONIX:**
  - ○ The JSC was interested in working with the publishing community because of their ONIX publishing protocol. The result of the collaboration, the RDA/ONIX framework, released in 2006, addresses the issue of resource categorization, and resulted in the proposal for Content, Media, and Carrier designations in RDA (http://www.rda-jsc.org/rdaonixann. html). ONIX (Online Information Exchange) is a metadata scheme used to describe and exchange publisher data in an automated environment.

2007

In October 2007, a further move toward the FRBR-ization of RDA took place when the JSC announced the rules would be restructured to reflect FRBR. The new format abandoned the familiar AACR2 organization and instead divided content into ten sections following FRBR concepts (JSC 2007).

2008

Shortly thereafter, in January 2008, "On the Record," the report of the Working Group on the Future of Bibliographic Control, was released. The group included academic librarians, representatives from the American Library Association, the American Association of Law Libraries, the Association of Research Libraries, the Special Libraries Association, Google, Microsoft, and the Program for Cooperative Cataloging (PCC). The Working Group was convened by the Library of Congress and asked to explore bibliographic control in light of changes in technology and library practice. When their report was released, recommendation 3.2.5 was "Suspend Work on RDA" (Library of Congress Working Group 2008, 29). The group suggested work should cease until a business case for RDA was articulated and problems already cited (such as readability, language, and ease of use) were addressed.

In response, the Library of Congress met with the National Library of Medicine and the National Agricultural Library in March 2008. The outcome of that meeting was a joint announcement on May 1, 2008, that the national libraries supported completion of RDA and would form the U.S. RDA Test Coordinating Committee to organize a test upon its completion. The test would cover the question of a business case (Marcum 2008).

The year 2008 ended with the long-awaited release of a final draft of RDA. It was made available in Portable Document Format (PDF). Unfortunately, *RDA Toolkit*, the online tool being designed for RDA, would not be ready for review until June 2010.

2

RDA History Since 2008

As stated in the previous chapter, in response to the call by "On the Record" to suspend work on RDA, the three U.S. national libraries issued a joint statement announcing the formation of the U.S. RDA Test Coordinating Committee.

GOALS FOR U.S. RDA TEST

The committee was charged to "devise and conduct a national test" that would:

- Evaluate RDA within the library and information environment
- Assess the technical, operational, and financial implications of implementing RDA, and
- Articulate the business case for RDA, including benefits to libraries and end users, along with cost analyses. (U.S. RDA Test Coordinating Committee 2011, 1)

TEST PARTICIPANTS: FORMAL AND INFORMAL

The U.S. RDA Test Coordinating Committee received over ninety-five applicants to participate in the national test and selected twenty-three of them. The committee strove to include a representative slice of libraries in their selection and considered the size and type of libraries, what systems they used, and what formats they cataloged, in making their decisions. The successful applicants along with the three national libraries made a total of twenty-six test partners.

In addition, the Coordinating Committee created a category of informal testers in response to the high amount of interest expressed in the test process. Any library, organization, or individual who wished could participate in this manner.

SUMMARY OF FINDINGS

The major findings of the final report, released in June 2011, are summarized here.

- Support for RDA:
  o There was overall support for implementing RDA.
  o Many believed changes were needed for a successful implementation.
- RDA and library technology:
  o RDA would work with current library systems.
  o RDA and MARC did not play particularly well together. A replacement for MARC would allow for a fuller implementation of RDA.
- Time to create RDA records:
  o Comparing RDA and AACR2 record creation times initially suggested there would be an increase in time needed to catalog with the new rules, but other results indicated there would be no time difference. Overall, RDA records would take about 30 minutes to create once catalogers were comfortable with it.
- Input from library catalog users:
  o 86% of respondents felt that RDA records met their needs.
  o 42% of respondents believed AACR2 and RDA records were about the same.
- Difficulties with *Toolkit*:
  o Test participants found the first version of *RDA Toolkit* difficult to use.
- RDA content:
  o RDA was a difficult text to work with and not easy to use.
  o Analysis suggested it required a college or graduate school reading ability.

As for the business case, the committee concluded that, "The test revealed that there is little discernible immediate benefit in implementing RDA alone." However, because of their strong belief in the potential future benefits of RDA, the Coordinating Committee recommended implementing RDA, "premised on the expectation that the problems uncovered by the test will be addressed as part of the preparation for implementation" (U.S. RDA Test Coordinating Committee 2011, 4).

RECOMMENDATIONS

In making their recommendations, the committee compared their test results to the ten stated goals for RDA (JSC, "Strategic Plan"). They judged that half of the goals were fully or partially met. Three goals were not met, one goal was outside the scope of the test, and another was not verified by the test findings. The Test Committee found that RDA was not written in plain English, was not easy or efficient to use, and its online version (the *Toolkit*) was problematic.

Based on the test findings, the committee's report offered nine recommendations, falling within six main categories.

RDA Content
1. Rewrite (reword) the RDA instructions.

RDA Toolkit
2. Define a process for updating the *Toolkit*.
3. Improve *Toolkit* functionality.
4. Develop full RDA examples in multiple schema to be available in the *Toolkit*.

RDA, Metadata, the Semantic Web, and Linked Data
5. Announce completion of the Registered RDA Elements Sets and Vocabularies.

RDA and [not] MARC
6. Demonstrate progress in developing a replacement for MARC RDA.

Training and Community Involvement
7. Encourage community involvement.
8. Coordinate RDA training nationally with LC, PCC, ALCTS, and others.

RDA and Library Technology
9. Encourage vendors and others to develop prototype input and discovery systems that use the RDA element set.

AFTER THE TEST: JUNE 2011–MARCH 2013

Work on the report's recommendations began almost immediately following their release. The committee provided three progress updates, in January and June 2012, and January 2013. Key achievements toward fulfillment of the committee's recommendations were reported. In January 2013, implementation of RDA was endorsed (U.S. RDA Test Coordinating Committee 2013, 1). Among the major changes that convinced the committee to recommend implementation was the editing and rewording of RDA chapters 6, 9, 10, 11, and 17 and effective *Toolkit* improvements. In addition, a schedule for RDA revisions was delivered. RDA will be updated four times per year, with three releases and an annual update. The releases may contain approved "fast track" changes and updated LC-PCC policies. The annual April update will contain more substantive changes agreed to by the JSC at their November meetings.

On March 2, 2012, the Library of Congress announced that they and their partner libraries planned to implement RDA on March 31, 2013

(Library of Congress, "Long-Range RDA Training" 2012). The Library of Congress used the year to complete training for its staff. RDA cataloging was fully implemented by the library on their target date.

For other libraries, there is no official start date for RDA. Libraries are free to plan their own implementation strategy to best suit their purposes. Libraries have chosen a variety of timelines and paths. Some decided to implement cataloging at the same time as LC; others waited to begin looking at RDA until after LC's start date. Still others have opted for a gradual approach to RDA, taking it in stages as they can.

3

Planning for RDA

The rollout for RDA, in contrast to AACR2, was planned as an extended process rather than a cold turkey start date for all. Library of Congress (LC) has been doing all of its original cataloging in RDA since April 2013. Other libraries have the option to adopt RDA when and as they can. While most libraries (perhaps all) have encountered RDA records by now, some (perhaps many) are still somewhere in the middle of implementing it in full. Under these circumstances, it is difficult to know how to approach a chapter on planning for RDA. I have opted to begin at the beginning and work from there. Although some readers will have dealt with a portion of the issues laid out here, others will be just gearing up to look at them.

Implementing a new cataloging code is a complex task that requires the support and commitment of administration and communication across all areas of the library. The process is likely to evolve rather than proceed in linear fashion. You should expect to adjust, change, and add to your plans as you go. This chapter looks at RDA from an organizational and training perspective. It addresses three major topics to consider when planning for RDA.

1. Training:
   o Determine how much RDA your cataloging staff needs, including decisions on the *RDA Toolkit* and FRBR background.
2. Inclusion:
   o Reach out to other functional areas impacted by RDA.
3. Time, Cost, and Impact Estimate:
   o Estimate the time needed for staff training and full implementation.

○ Work with others in your library to ensure that RDA training causes minimal disruption in other services.
○ Determine the hard and soft costs involved.

TRAINING

The biggest step in implementing RDA is, of course, training for your resource management team. Whether you decide on a formal training program with classroom hours and exercises, opt for an ad hoc approach where staff learn as they go, or some combination of the two, it will be important to identify what needs to be learned and who needs to learn which bits of it.

A good place to start is to look at your staffing levels and organization and to analyze your department workflows—cataloging, acquisitions, authority work, and database maintenance. (Libraries involved with non-MARC metadata creation will have additional training requirements, which are outside the scope of this book.) Determine exactly what your library does for resource management and what level of expertise they employ in doing it. This will help you determine which staff need what kind of training and how much.

As you plan to implement RDA, keep your analysis of workflows in mind and be on the lookout for opportunities to improve them. *There is no better time to introduce changes to existing workflows than during a time of great change.*

Copy Cataloging and Acquisitions

If your library gets most of its bibliographic records from outside sources and does little local editing, then your staff may only require a basic familiarity with RDA. Your library may fit this level if you belong to a consortium that provides centralized cataloging or if you receive and accept MARC records "as they are" from your materials vendors. A minimal approach to RDA training in this situation could be simply learning how to recognize RDA records.

If your library's cataloging activity consists primarily of finding records from an outside source (bibliographic utility, vendor, or z39.50 service) and editing them to reflect local preferences, then you want to concentrate training on copy cataloging rather than original cataloging. Libraries that perform local editing need to adjust their copy workflows to accommodate RDA changes. They need to know where RDA differs from AACR2 and which RDA rules specify the changes. Libraries and staff at this level need to review the kind of local editing they perform and check whether RDA requires changes in what they do. Major changes introduced in RDA as well as how the changes are mapped into MARC should be investigated.

Training for staff who will revise your documentation on copy-cataloging policies should include an introduction to RDA's content as well as its structure and FRBR terminology. A close study of RDA's text is perhaps not necessary but an ability to locate the rules that lead to the changes is. In some organizations, copy catalogers will be included in this process; in others they won't. In the latter situations, training for copy catalogers might simply focus on reviewing updated policies and documentation with them.

It's important to note that for copy cataloging, RDA workflows may exist parallel to AACR2 workflows. Because RDA is backwards compatible, existing AACR2 records can remain in library databases and do not have to be updated to RDA. Libraries have the option to continue to keep and use AACR2 records according to AACR2 rules at the same time that they create, import, and use RDA records per RDA rules. Thus, copy catalogers will inhabit a mixed environment and must be versatile in handling both kinds of records.

In addition, the library community has offered guidelines for adding RDA elements to AACR2 records. These records, known as hybrid records, will retain their status and coding as AACR2 records, but may contain RDA data. Your library will need to decide whether you want to always, sometimes, or never enhance AACR2 records this way.

Acquisitions librarians are often responsible for importing bibliographic records into a library's database at the point of ordering. Depending on a library's workflow, these records may be short vendor-supplied records or fuller records imported from a bibliographic utility and edited. In many libraries, staff working outside of cataloging add these records. Depending on your library's workflow, acquisitions librarians may need to be included in copy cataloging training.

Original and Complex Copy Cataloging

For libraries or staff members who perform complex copy cataloging and original cataloging, more extensive learning in RDA should be provided. Original catalogers need to be familiar with RDA's organization and content as well as the tools used to access them.

Topics to be familiar with will include:

- FRBR and FRAD conceptual models
- RDA's structure and terminology
- RDA's objectives and principles—covered in RDA's introductory chapter (chapter 0)
- RDA elements and relationships, and how they translate to MARC fields
- RDA Core elements (chapter 0.6) and the additional LC Core elements
- Major changes between AACR2 and RDA
- *RDA Toolkit* navigation and use, if purchased

Special-Format Cataloging

Additional training is needed for catalogers who work with special formats such as maps, music, religious, and legal resources. Unlike AACR2, RDA does not have separate chapters to cover separate formats. Rather, instructions for special formats are interwoven into the rules for each element. When there is a specific rule for a certain format it is given within the chapter covering that element. For example, recording dimensions of maps is included in chapter 3.5 with all the other directions about dimensions.

The change from designated chapters to inclusion in general rules means there is no single place in RDA where all the changes for a specific format are listed. This makes it difficult for catalogers to be confident that they are aware of them all.

Authority Work and Database Management

If your library does its own authority maintenance or uses an authority vendor to update headings, RDA changes both the concepts and vocabulary used in authority work. Authority librarians need to become comfortable with the FRAD conceptual model and its impact on RDA.

In addition to changes in how new authorities are constructed, there may be retrospective cleanup needed for existing records as a result of some of RDA's changes. Authority librarians will need to plan whether your database requires corrections, and how best to do it. Some of the work may be automated in batch processes, but some will require one-by-one manual correction.

Authority librarians also need to be aware that a suite of new fields has been added to the MARC Authority Formats. The fields offer an opportunity to enhance the information provided in an authority record. Because they are not all core elements, libraries may make local decisions on when to add the data.

The Program for Cooperative Programming's NACO program has been very active in exploring RDA issues for authority records. Your library will need to stay abreast of its role in updating records in the national authority files.

Do You Need the *RDA Toolkit*?

Libraries will have to decide whether or not to purchase the *RDA Toolkit*. For libraries whose cataloging activity consists chiefly of copy cataloging, it is probably possible to get away without it. However, having a subscription will make learning and using RDA much easier. The *Toolkit* enables navigation within RDA and offers context-sensitive links to both AACR2 rules and LC-PCC (Library of Congress–Program for Cooperative Cataloging)

Policy Statements. In addition, the *Toolkit* includes mapping information for MARC encoding. These features make it an attractive option if it is a possibility for your library.

Much has been written about the financial burden that the *RDA Toolkit* subscription model places on libraries, and there is no doubt that its cost will be a problem for some libraries. To help in the decision process, libraries can consider the following points:

- Take advantage of ALA Publishing's trial *Toolkit* offer.
  - ○ The trial can help your library to see how necessary or appropriate it is for you.
- Consider a subscription for your initial implementation year.
  - ○ Reassess at renewal time.
- Review your other subscriptions and library tools.
  - ○ Have any fallen out of use or become available in other resources?
- Be aware that there is a publicly accessible part of the *Toolkit.*
  - ○ Visitors will find sample record sets and the LC-PCC Policy Statements.
- Keep in mind that print RDA now has an update schedule.
  - ○ Revised print editions of the rules will be regularly released.

And remember, if your library decides for financial or other reasons not to invest in the *Toolkit,* the print or eBook versions can be viable alternatives.

FRBR and FRAD

Finally, when assessing your library's training needs for RDA, recognize that some background in FRBR and FRAD will be necessary. Assess your staff's familiarity with these conceptual models and provide basic or review training for those who need it. A quick look at RDA's table of contents and a perusal of just about any paragraph of its text will convince you that learning RDA will go a lot easier if you learn a bit about FRBR and FRAD first.

INCLUSION

Once you have an idea of who needs what training in your resource management department, you can broaden the discussion to other library functions, including public services, systems, and budgeting. Identify a core group of people who represent these areas and let them know that RDA has been implemented nationally and is in the process of being implemented in your library. Representatives from these departments can provide input on how RDA will impact them and can help you determine how best to include them in the library's implementation process.

All libraries should expect that RDA will impact their budgets, their library systems (both back and front ends), and their interactions with library services vendors. Decisions about an *RDA Toolkit* subscription will need to be made in collaboration with administration. Changes in MARC fields will impact your library system with issues about indexing on the back end as well as display and searching in the public-facing interfaces (your OPAC or Discovery layer). Both your systems staff and public services staff should be involved in decisions on how you handle these issues. It is also important to communicate with outsourced services vendors to ask whether your (or their) RDA implementation will impact workflows that are currently working between the two of you. There may be additional financial impacts with library services vendors as they adjust to RDA as well.

In summary, the following groups should be included in your RDA preparations:

- Administration, Finance—Cost of *RDA Toolkit*, other vendor changes
- Systems—Prepare library systems for RDA, including ILS, online catalog, and discovery layer
- Public Services—Display and searching changes
- Vendors—Coordinate impact of RDA between the library and its vendors

An additional consideration here is whether to provide RDA training to staff in other functional areas of the library. In some cases, it may be necessary. In others, it could help build acceptance and goodwill. Some possibilities include:

- Acquisitions librarians not in Tech Services
  - Training in copy cataloging
- Public Services librarians
  - Should know about changes in public catalog displays and search capabilities due to RDA
- Systems librarians
  - Need to know how changed and new MARC fields will impact system configuration and maintenance
- All staff
  - Might appreciate a general overview of RDA and its most visible changes

ESTIMATE TIME, COST, AND IMPACT

You might also want to estimate how much RDA is going to cost in terms of time and money. Training needs and local impact were certainly major concerns in the U.S. library community while RDA was being developed. It was also a focus of the U.S. RDA Test Coordinating Committee.

Training Time from RDA Test Findings

The committee asked test participants to estimate how much time might be needed to train key trainers who could then train remaining staff (U.S. RDA Test Coordinating Committee 2011, 108). While there were not an overwhelming number of responses, those received seemed to agree that 15 to 40 hours was realistic.

Test participants were also asked how much training would be required for other staff. Of the twelve libraries that replied, more than half gave answers that fell within the 30 to 50 hours range. Training was seen to encompass classroom hours or a combination of classroom sessions, practice, and discussions/meetings (U.S. RDA Test Coordinating Committee 2011, 109).

The test committee also tried to determine a learning curve for RDA. When participants were asked how long it would take for staff to "produce acceptable RDA records," estimates fell within a 1–12 months range (U.S. RDA Test Coordinating Committee 2011, 109). Another measure for the learning curve came from the time data collected by the committee. For the test participants themselves, the time needed to create an RDA record fell from 53 minutes at the beginning of the test to 26 minutes shortly thereafter (U.S. RDA Test Coordinating Committee 2011, 46).

What can be concluded from this information? Test participants agreed that, whether key trainer or other staff, somewhere between 15 and 50 hours of learning would be needed to become comfortable with RDA. In addition, the learning curve for producing RDA records may be less than a year, while the time to create an RDA record quickly becomes an acceptable 26 minutes in short order.

Training Materials and Tools

There are many options for what kind of training you will employ. Your choice will depend on your particular staff needs, learning preferences, and your budget. Whatever decisions are made, be sure to include both the hard and soft costs involved in your planning.

Impact on Library

One of the most difficult aspects of providing training is balancing its necessity with other obligations. While it is difficult to assess whether your implementation will result in backlogs in cataloging or other areas, it is something you should think about when planning. Even if you can't say for sure it will happen, it is good to include a conversation about the possibility in your discussions. Similarly, if attending a workshop or training session means staff can't cover other responsibilities at that time, be sure to alert those areas impacted. You will need to provide alternative coverage solutions to avoid holes in service.

CONCLUSION

We have now looked at overarching organizational issues to consider when deciding on your RDA implementation plan. You should identify which of your staff members need to learn what, and to what level of expertise. In addition, plan to involve people from other areas of the library in your planning. For certain, you will need the help of your systems department and the cooperation of public services. In addition, administrators should be aware of the costs involved in the effort. These include hard costs, such as a *Toolkit* subscription or the cost of a training webinar. In addition, staff time spent training is a soft cost that needs to be considered.

The next chapter looks at some of the main implementation issues you will encounter as you introduce RDA to your library.

Implementation Issues

The last chapter discussed training issues for RDA. This chapter turns its attention to some of the larger implementation concerns involved in introducing the new standard.

YOUR LEGACY DATA—BIBLIOGRAPHIC RECORDS

RDA is designed to create bibliographic data that are compatible with records created under AACR2 and earlier cataloging codes. The JSC intended for RDA records to coexist with AACR2 records (RDA 0.2). Hence, libraries do not need to update their existing AACR2 records to comply with RDA.

Even so, some libraries (and in some cases the larger community) are choosing to update records in certain instances. The *Report of the PCC Post-Implementation Hybrid Bibliographic Records Guidelines Task Group* compiled a list of changes that could likely be effected via automated batch processes (PCC 2012, 19–20). Hybrid records are AACR2 records that are enhanced with selected RDA elements and practices, but that retain their AACR2 coding. The PCC list included:

- 245: Remove the General Material Designator (GMD)—245 subfield h (but PCC recommends not before March 31, 2016)
- 245 subfield c: Remove ellipses and change Latin abbreviation (". . . [et al.]" becomes "[and others]")
- 260: Substitute spelled-out English equivalents for Latin abbreviations in the 260 field, for example, "[Place of publication not identified]" replaces "[S.l.]"

- 260, subfield c: Replace lowercase c or p with copyright or phonogram symbols © and ℗ before a date
- 300: Spell out abbreviations and change Latin abbreviations to English equivalents, for example, p. becomes pages, v. becomes volumes
- 300: Change designations from AACR2 terms to RDA terms when they differ, for example, sound disc to audio disc, sound cassette to audiocassette
- 336, 337, and 338: Add these fields, including subfields a, b, and 2

Libraries may decide to make some of these changes at their local level. Their ability to do so depends on having the necessary tools, expertise, and staff time.

In addition, bibliographic utilities have made changes to their services or to their records to address RDA issues. OCLC continues to use batch processes to hybridize AACR2 records where possible (OCLC 2013). Their changes reflect the PCC report and include:

- Add 336, 337, 338 fields
- Spell out appropriate abbreviations in 255, 300, 500, 504, and other fields
- Convert Latin abbreviations to English equivalents in 245, 260, and other fields
- Convert dissertation notes in 502 field to multiple subfields

Changes by the utilities will not change your local records, but will impact your local policy decisions.

YOUR LEGACY DATA—AUTHORITY HEADINGS

RDA is also meant to be backward compatible with AACR2 authority headings (known as authorized access points in RDA). There are several candidates for local updating that have been made in the LC/NACO Authority File already (PCC-LC 2012, 7–9). NACO is the PCC's Name Authority Cooperative Program. Member libraries contribute authority records to the national authority file. Among the changes that have been made are these:

- Bible. $p O.T. changed to Bible. $p Old Testament
- Bible. $p N.T. changed to Bible. $p New Testament
- Bible. $p [O.T. or N.T.] $p [Book of Bible] changed to Bible. $p [Book]
  - o For example, Bible. $p Corinthians
- Koran changed to Qu'ran
- Dept. changed to Department

Other changes made to the LC/NACO Authority File are:

- Violincello changed to cello
- "ca." changed to approximately
- "fl." changed to active
- "cent." changed to century

- Months spelled out (Jan. changed to January)
- Birth or death dates designated with hyphens before/after date, instead of with preceding abbreviations "b." and "d." (b. 2014 becomes 2014 -)

Whether and how you upgrade existing AACR2 authorized headings into RDA authorized access points in your bibliographic records depends on how you currently deal with authority work. If your library works with an authorities vendor to maintain your authority files, then you probably have a process in place for updating access points in your bibliographic files. Some libraries do not maintain a separate authority file, and others send their bibliographic database for periodic updating to authority vendors.

The Program for Cooperative Cataloging (PCC) has played a crucial role in identifying changes needed in the LC/NACO Authority File headings to be RDA compliant. They have employed a three-step process. The changes listed above were largely done in Phase 2. Phase 3 will attempt to upgrade the remaining 7.5 million authority records not yet verified as RDA compliant (PCC March 2014, 1).

LOCAL POLICY FOR NEW RECORDS

Libraries now get catalog records from a variety of sources.

- Copy cataloging from:
  o Bibliographic utilities (OCLC, SkyRiver)
  o Your library services platform "cloud" (Ex Libris/Alma's community zone)
  o A z39.50 search tool (from LC or other libraries)
- Creating original records
- Batch loading records from materials vendors (YBP, B&T, OverDrive, etc.)

RDA necessitates a review of policies and processes for them all.

Copy Cataloging Issues

- What kinds of records will you accept in your catalog?
  o Only RDA records
  o Only AACR2 records, until further notice
  o RDA, Hybrid, and AACR2 records
- Editing Policy Options
  o Always upgrade AACR2 records to RDA as part of copy cataloging?
  o Enhance AACR2 records with a specific set of RDA elements as a matter of course (e.g., always add 33x fields?)?
  o Edit AACR2 records according to AACR2 rules, with no enhancements; edit RDA records according to RDA.

- Documentation Updates
  - o Maintain AACR2 editing policies, with or without instructions for hybridizing with RDA elements.
    - Use in parallel with RDA policies?
  - o Develop RDA policies that reflect RDA's changes for different formats.
    - Decide to upgrade all records to RDA and maintain only RDA documentation?

Original Cataloging

When the Library of Congress moved to RDA-only cataloging in April 2013, many libraries began to tackle RDA's copy cataloging issues, planning to address original cataloging later. Because the prospect of RDA can be so daunting, a phased approach is a good way to go. Starting with copy cataloging provides an opportunity to get a sense of what RDA looks like in MARC and highlights some of the biggest changes from AACR2. Copy cataloging, therefore, builds a good base from which to tackle original cataloging. In addition to the major issues and time involved in training for RDA (discussed in chapter 3), the nuts and bolts of original cataloging in RDA will require local policy decisions on three important parts of RDA.

- Decisions on core requirements
- Decisions on alternative and optional omissions/additions
- Decisions on LC-PCC Policy Statements

Core Requirements

RDA establishes a core-level record standard by identifying a minimal set of required elements. The Library of Congress has enhanced RDA's core elements with "LC core elements." Your library is required to meet the RDA core standard, but may opt to follow LC's enhanced core level.

Alternatives and Options

There are also many places in RDA where alternative instructions or options are offered. Libraries may decide to apply these on a case-by-case basis, or review the alternatives and options ahead of time and make blanket local policy decisions on each.

LC-PCC Policy Statements

RDA is enhanced with policy statements from both the Library of Congress (LC) and the Program for Cooperative Cataloging (PCC). At the local level, libraries should decide when they follow RDA, when LC, and when PCC. This can be done as a blanket policy or by making separate decisions for each statement.

Implementation Timeline

Libraries may want to decide on an implementation timeline and perhaps set a target date for moving to RDA for original cataloging. As noted earlier, there is no end-of-life date for AACR2 and presumably libraries may continue to use the rules for as long as they like. Even so, the community impetus is toward RDA. The PCC BIBCO program (the Monographic Bibliographic Record Cooperative Program) announced at ALA Midwinter 2014 that its partner libraries would catalog in RDA from January 1, 2015 (PCC February 2014, 1). BIBCO is a group of fifty or so libraries that cooperatively contribute original monographic records to international databases, including the Library of Congress (LC) catalog. In LC, these records are identified as "pcc" in the MARC 042 field.

Vendor Records and Batch Loads

Receiving files of records from materials vendors has become increasingly popular for both electronic and print materials in recent years. The files are usually loaded by a batch method. Libraries have developed various approaches to reviewing and editing these records, sometimes making global changes and, less often, opting for manual corrections. Many libraries use tools available in their library services platform, or other editing tools, to revise, update, or correct records in batch mode. When it comes to loading records into the local database, most library systems have some kind of loader process or table that must be edited to specify how data in the incoming records are mapped into your database.

Hence, there are three parts to your approach to RDA and vendor files. You need to work with your vendor to find out how they are introducing RDA into the files you are receiving from them. You should check your preprocessing policies to see if you need to add, update, or change anything to accommodate RDA. Finally, review your loading process and make changes as necessary.

- Communicate with vendor regarding their plans for RDA:
  - What is their timeline for providing RDA records?
  - Do they already provide a mix of RDA, AACR2, and hybrid records?
- Review your preprocessing and your loading process for the files:
  - Do you need to add or change anything because of RDA?

GMD AND 33X FIELDS

The demise of the General Material Designation (GMD) in the MARC 245 subfield 'h' has been one of RDA's more controversial changes. Librarians and patrons alike are used to scanning results lists and using the GMD to identify formats, for example, [electronic resource] or [sound recording].

The GMD was replaced with three new fields for content (MARC 336), media (MARC 337), and carrier (MARC 338). While the terms taken in combination technically describe a resource's format(s), the terms cannot be said to be user friendly. For instance, a book is designated as content text, carrier volume, and media unmediated.

Systems vendors have been slow to utilize the 33x fields. While most have added the fields to their MARC tables, many have not introduced ways to productively display them in OPACs and discovery layers. In turn, libraries have been loath to abandon the GMD in favor of displaying unfriendly 33x terms in their catalogs. Some libraries will add the GMD to RDA records until such time as systems come up with good display options for 3xx fields. The PCC recommendations for hybrid records favor retaining GMDs in hybrid records, even when 33x fields are added, until March 31, 2016 (PCC 2012, 6).

You can see that there are multiple issues to be decided at the local level.

- Will your library add GMDs to RDA records?
- Will your library retain 33x fields in RDA records, if adding GMDs?
- Will your library add 33x fields to AACR2 records as part of hybridization?
- System issues:
  o Does your library system's MARC tables validate the 33x MARC fields?
  o Does your library system index the 33x fields? As keyword or otherwise?
  o Does your discovery layer use the 33x fields in its faceting in any way?
- Do your OPAC or discovery layers display the 33x fields to the public?
  o Do you have the option to manipulate the display to make it useful to patrons?
  o Can you prevent 33x displays in the public catalogs?

At some future time, when library catalogs and discovery layers are using the 33x fields in a useful way, libraries may need to address whether to delete GMDs from their AACR2 records and add 33x fields to them (if not already done).

RELATIONSHIP DESIGNATORS FOR 1XX, 7XX

PCC Guidelines for the Application of Relationship Designators in Bibliographic Records calls for the use of relationship designators for all creators and recommends their use for contributors and others. The PCC Post-Implementation Hybrid Bibliographic Records Guidelines Task Force report includes relationship designators as RDA elements that can be added to AACR2 records.

- Will your library add relationship designators to any appropriate access points in RDA records, or will you limit their use to creators?
- Will you enhance AACR2 records with relationship designators for creators only, or for other access points as well?

- Will you enter relationship designator terms from RDA's appendices (subfield 'e'), enter only relationship designator codes from the MARC Code List for Relators (subfield '4'), or include both?
- System issues:
  - Does your library system recognize the relationship subfields in the MARC tables/validation?
  - Are the subfields indexed?
  - Do they affect searching or display in the public catalog(s)?

MARC 264 FIELD

During RDA's implementation, use of the Publication, Distribution, etc. (Imprint) MARC 260 field was replaced with the Production, Publication, Distribution, Manufacture, and Copyright Notice MARC 264 field to provide a coded way to differentiate between production (unpublished), publication, distribution, manufacture, and copyright information. Your library has a couple of local decisions to make.

- Libraries may enhance an AACR2 record by converting a 260 field to a 264 field, if desired, per the PCC hybridization guidelines (PCC 2012, 11).
- In RDA records, libraries should use a copyright date [in brackets] as a publication date per the LC-PCC Policy Statement at 2.8.6.6. They can optionally record the copyright date in a separate 264 _4 $c field. LC does not require it, but many libraries are doing so.

CONCLUSION

We have looked at some of the major issues to be addressed when implementing RDA. Your library will need to make decisions about:

- Updating legacy AACR2 bibliographic data
- Updating legacy AACR2 authority data
- Revising copy cataloging practices to include RDA and hybrid records
- Training and implementation for original cataloging, including
  - Your library's "core level"
  - Policies regarding RDA alternatives and options
  - LC-PCC Policy Statements
- GMD and MARC 33x issues
- Use of relationship designators
- RDA and LC policies on use of the MARC 264 field

System issues are included in the topics above, but it is perhaps worthwhile to collocate and repeat them here. In preparing for RDA, you will need to be in touch with your system administrators and with your library services platform vendor. Some of the issues that will come up include:

- Loader configurations, tables
- MARC field tables and validation
- Indexing and facets search and limit impacts
- OPAC and discovery layer display issues (e.g., 33x fields)

The next chapter looks at the foundations of RDA, the Functional Requirements for Bibliographic Records (FRBR) and for Authority Data (FRAD).

FRBR, FRAD, and RDA

In this chapter we lay the groundwork for RDA training and implementation. Having noted that a familiarity with FRBR and FRAD are necessary, we start with a review of these conceptual models. We then look at how FRBR and FRAD are "translated" into RDA and how they are incorporated into RDA's basic organization.

FRBR AND FRAD

FRBR and FRAD are projects of the International Federation of Library Associations and Institutions (IFLA). IFLA's Study Group on Functional Requirements for Bibliographic Records (FRBR) began work in 1992, and its final report appeared in 1998. The Working Group on Functional Requirements and Numbering of Authority Records (FRANAR) was established in 1999. Its draft report *Functional Requirements for Authority Data: A Conceptual Model* (FRAD) came out in April 2007 and was approved in March 2009.

Both FRBR and FRAD are based on entity-relationship analysis and are best described as conceptual models for organizing data. In the conceptual model, components of bibliographic and authority data are:

- Identified as *entities*,
- Described by *attributes*, and then,
- *Related* to each other.

Another important point is that FRBR and FRAD define sets of user tasks that their data is designed to satisfy. There is some overlap between the two because bibliographic and authority data serve somewhat the same, but sometimes different, purposes. (See FRBR and FRAD User Tasks)

FRBR and FRAD User Tasks

FRBR User Tasks	FRAD User Tasks
1. Find	1. Find
2. Identify	2. Identify
3. Select	3. Contextualize ("Clarify" in RDA)
4. Obtain	4. Justify ("Understand" in RDA)

Functional Requirements for Bibliographic Records—FRBR

FRBR defines three groups of entities. (See FRBR's Three Entity Groups)

Group 1: Primary entities (WEMI)
- Work: "A distinct intellectual or artistic creation"
- Expression: "The specific intellectual or artistic form that a work takes"
- Manifestation: "The physical embodiment of an expression of a work"
- Item: "A single exemplar of a manifestation"

Group 2: Entities responsible for Group 1 entities (P, F, Cb)
- Person
- Corporate body
- Family (added by FRAD)

Group 3: Subjects of Group 1 entities (COPE+)
- Concept
- Object
- Place
- Event
- + All Group 1 and Group 2 entities can also be subjects

FRBR's Three Entity Groups

			Entities
Group 1 (Primary)	RESOURCES	Products of intellectual or artistic endeavors	WEMI = Work, Expression, Manifestation, Item
Group 2	CREATORS	Those responsible for producing Group One entities	P, F, Cb = Person, Family, Corporate body
Group 3	SUBJECTS	Subjects of intellectual or artistic endeavors	COPE+ = Concept, Object, Place, Event + WEMI + P, F, Cb

Functional Requirements for Authority Data—FRAD

FRAD builds on the FRBR model to show that bibliographic entities from FRBR can be "known as" a name or be "assigned" a unique identifier. These names or identifiers become the basis for controlled access points. (See Arrow Diagram)

Arrow Diagram for High-Level FRAD Model

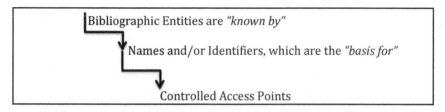

In FRAD, "name" is an entity, and includes personal names, corporate names, names of families, trade names, titles of works and manifestations, and names of concepts, objects, events, and places (IFLA 2013, 24). In FRBR, "title" and "name" were attributes. The change allows for differentiation, or relationships, between, say, a person and the name(s) that the person is known by.

An expanded diagram of the FRAD model adds two relationships and entities to the modelmodel (See Expanded FRAD Diagram). Controlled access points have a *created by whom* relationship with an agency and an *according to what* relationship with the rules used to construct them.

Expanded FRAD Diagram

	• FRBR Entities		
Bibliographic Entities	Group 1: Work Expression Manifestation Item	Group 2: Person Family Corporate body	Group 3: Concept Object Place Event
	Known by/Assigned:		
Authority Entities	• Names • Identifiers		
	Used to construct (Is Basis For):		
	• Controlled Access Points		
	By whom:	*According to what:*	
	• Agency	• Rules	

Relationships

Relationships form the second half of both the FRBR and FRAD entity-relationship conceptual models. The FRBR relationships deal with such bibliographic topics as the relationship of a work to its subject or an author to his or her work. The FRAD relationships deal with familiar authority concepts such as the relationship between a name and a pseudonym, or that between a title in Spanish and the same title in English. FRBR and FRAD, by naming relationships, provide a means by which to make them explicit.

FRBR Relationships

FRBR identifies four main groups of bibliographic relationships. Section 5.2, "Relationships Depicted in the High-Level Diagram," covers three kinds of relationship groups. Section 5.3, "Other Relationships Between Group 1 Entities," describes the fourth. These relationships are recorded as bibliographic data.

5.2.1 Relationships Between Work, Expression, Manifestation, and Item

FRBR refers to these group 1 relationships as high-level and logical relationships. They are the "realized through," "embodied in," and "exemplified by" relationships that tie any single work to its expression, and in turn to its manifestation and then item. These relationships are inherent in a resource. If you have an item in hand, by definition it contains all four levels of bibliographic identity. It contains an item, a manifestation, an expression, and a work.

5.2.2 Relationships (of Works) to Persons and Corporate Bodies (and Families)

The second group of entities—persons, corporate bodies, and families (added later by FRAD)—is related to group 1 entities (WEMIs) through the "created by (for a work)," "realized by (for an expression)," "produced by (for a manifestation)," and "owned by (for an item)" relationships.

5.2.3 Subject Relationships

Any of the entities in FRBR's three groups can be related via a "has as subject" relationship to a work. Turned around, a work may have as its subject any of the FRBR entities—another work, an expression, a manifestation, or an item (group 1); a person, corporate body, or family (group 2); or it may be about a concept, object, place, or event (group 3).

5.3 Other Relationships Between Group 1 Entities

FRBR's sections 5.3.1 to 5.3.6 describe commonly found relationships between different works, expressions, manifestations, and items. For example, FRBR's Table 5.1 describes work-to-work relationships, including a "successor" relationship (e.g., a sequel) and an "imitation" relationship (e.g., a parody).

FRBR's list of relationships is not exhaustive (but is exhausting to read through). In addition to work-to-work relationships, there are relationship tables for expression-to-expression, expression-to-work, manifestation-to-manifestation, manifestation-to-item, and item-to-item.

FRAD Relationships

FRAD categorizes four additional groups of relationships that, in the current RDA MARC implementation, are depicted in various ways in authority records.

5.2 Relationships Depicted in the High-Level Diagrams

These are the relationships that operate between the three components of FRAD—the bibliographic entities, the names and identifiers by which they are known, and the controlled access points created to represent them. (See Expanded FRAD Diagram, p. 29)

The relationships are similar to FRBR's high-level diagram relationships in that there is only one relationship between any two entities, and it is inherent between them. For example, a controlled access point has the relationship "is basis for/is based on" with a name or an identifier.

5.3 Relationships between Persons, Families, Corporate Bodies, and Works

FRAD also describes relationships that can exist between persons, families, and corporate bodies, as well as relationships that can exist among works. The relationships can be between the following entities:

- Person to person
- Person to family
- Person to corporate body
- Family to family
- Family to corporate body
- Corporate body to corporate body
- Work to work

Many of the relationships described here are "structural" in nature, such as a person being a member of a corporate body or of a family, or a corporate body that is owned by another corporate body or by a family. Pseudonymous relationships are included in this category as person-to-person relationships. While the actual pseudonym is a name, the entity represented by the name is considered to be a persona (a person) in FRAD.

5.4 Relationships between the Various Names of Persons, Families, Corporate Bodies, and Works

Whereas the relationships in 5.3 deal with relationships between different entities (e.g., between two different families), the relationships in 5.4 deal with relationships between different forms of name for the same entity. These are the categories for which this type of relationship can exist:

- Name of person to name of person
- Name of family to name of family
- Name of corporate body to name of corporate body
- Name of work to name of work

Earlier and later names are examples of a name of person/name of person relationship.

5.5 Relationships between Controlled Access Points

In this final category, FRAD recognizes relationships between different controlled access points that represent the same entity. Examples of these relationships are controlled access points in parallel languages or alternate scripts, or controlled access points constructed under different rules for authority work.

FRBR AND FRAD IN RDA

RDA reflects the FRBR and FRAD models in a couple of essential ways. First, RDA's elements bear a direct correspondence to the entity attributes and relationships defined in FRBR and FRAD. Second, RDA's organization originates with the entities, relationships, and user tasks in FRBR and FRAD.

RDA Elements Correspond to FRBR and FRAD Attributes/Relationships

To understand how the JSC imported FRBR/FRAD concepts into RDA, it is good to look at the mapping charts available at their RDA website (JSC, "FRBR-RDA Mapping"). You can also view the Entity-Relationship Diagrams (ERD) available in the *RDA Toolkit*. The diagrams for core elements and relationships are available on the public portion of the *RDA Toolkit* as well as in the subscription product. (At the RDA Background page, http://www.rdatoolkit.org/background, scroll down to the Entity Relationship section.)

As an example, the FRBR attribute "Title of the manifestation" has multiple corresponding RDA elements, including "Title," "Title proper," "Parallel title proper," and "Variant title." (See JSC FRBR to RDA Mapping)

The JSC mapping chart makes explicit the correspondence of the single FRBR manifestation attribute "title" to multiple elements in RDA.

JSC FRBR to RDA Mapping for Title of the Manifestation

FRBR attribute/relationship	Corresponding RDA element
Attributes of manifestation	
4.4.1 Title of the manifestation	Title Title proper Parallel title proper Other title information Parallel other title information Variant title Earlier title proper Later title proper Key title Abbreviated title

(From JSC "FRBR to RDA Mapping", Used under Creative Commons Attribution 4.0 International License.)

RDA's Organization Reflects FRBR and FRAD

Entities and Relationships

RDA makes its connection to FRBR and FRAD very clear in its introductory chapter. Section 0.3 explicitly names the two conceptual models and explains RDA's alignment with each. Section 0.5 describes RDA's organization in terms of the two models. Following a similar order to FRBR and FRAD, RDA is presented in two parts; the first part (sections 1–4) deals with entities and their attributes, and the second part (sections 5–10) describes relationships between them.

User Tasks

The user tasks defined in FRBR and FRAD are also incorporated into RDA's organization. The opening lines of RDA's text on the FRBR user tasks (find, identify, select, and obtain) state that, "the data created using RDA to describe a resource are designed to assist users performing [these tasks]." Likewise, "data created using RDA to describe an entity associated with a resource are designed to assist users [with the FRAD tasks (find, identify, clarify, and understand)]" (RDA 0.0).

Expanding the connection further, RDA links each of its ten sections to specific user tasks. Every section begins with a chapter of general guidelines. The guidelines include "Functional Objectives and Principles" that cite the user tasks addressed in the section's chapters.

CONCLUSION

In this chapter, we built a foundation for understanding RDA by review-ing FRBR and FRAD. In the next few chapters we take a big-picture look at RDA itself, looking at its introductory chapter, its structure, and other tips for using the content standard.

6

RDA's Introductory Chapter

We have looked at RDA's history and development and reviewed its conceptual basis in FRBR and FRAD. Now we'll take a look at RDA itself. We begin with a look at RDA's basic structure and its introductory chapter.

RDA'S BASIC STRUCTURE

As has been noted, RDA is divided into ten sections that coordinate with the FRBR and FRAD entities and relationships. Sections 1–4 cover recording attributes of the entities. Sections 5–10 provide instructions on recording relationships between entities. Between them, the ten sections contain thirty-seven chapters. (See RDA's Basic Structure)

RDA's Basic Structure

RDA's Basic Structure		
0	Introduction	0
Recording Attributes of Entities		
Section	Section Title	Chapters
1	Recording Attributes of Manifestation & Item	1–4
2	Recording Attributes of Work & Expression	5–7
3	Recording Attributes of Person, Family, & Corporate Body	8–11
4	Recording Attributes of Concept, Object, Event, & Place	12–16
Recording Relationships		
Section	Section Title	Chapters
5	Recording **Primary Relationships Between** Work, Expressions, Manifestations, & Items	17
6	Recording **Relationships To** Persons, Families, & Corporate Bodies	18–22
7	Recording **Relationships To** Concepts, Objects, Events, & Places	23
8	Recording **Relationships Between** Works, Expressions, Manifestations, & Items	24–28
9	Recording **Relationships Between** Persons, Families, & Corporate Bodies	29–32
10	Recording **Relationships Between** Concepts, Objects, Events, & Places	33–37

RDA'S INTRODUCTORY CHAPTER

Before jumping into RDA's instructions, it is good advice to spend some time reading its introductory chapter. It offers insight into RDA's structure, principles, organization, and features, and can make using RDA easier. We will look at some of the more important points, but it is worth your while to read it through in full.

Objectives and Principles Governing Resource Description and Access (0.4)

RDA is based on a stated set of principles and objectives that are listed and defined at RDA 0.4.

RDA's objectives are outlined at 0.4.2.

- Responsiveness to user needs
- Cost efficiency
- Flexibility
- Continuity

RDA's principles are grounded in *The Statement of International Cataloguing Principles,* developed by the Meeting of Experts on an International Cataloging Code, organized by the International Federation of Library Associations and Institutions (IFLA 2009).

RDA's principles (0.4.3):

- Differentiation
- Sufficiency
- Relationships
- Representation
- Accuracy
- Attribution
- Common Usage or Practice
- Uniformity

Core Elements (0.6)

AACR2 defined three levels of description and defined a minimum set of elements to be included for each level (AACR2 1.0D). In contrast, RDA defines only a minimum-level record, identifying core elements that must be included when applicable.

A complete list of core elements is provided at 0.6, organized by RDA section. The general notes (0.6.1) explain that RDA's core elements were selected on the basis of their importance to specific user tasks. For bibliographic descriptions, the user tasks of identifying and selecting a manifestation, and identifying works and creators, were the key tasks for determining core element status. Core elements for relationships were selected based on the user tasks of finding (a person, family, or corporate body associated with a resource) and identifying (a person, family, or corporate body).

The April 2014 update to RDA included clarification at 0.6.1 about multiple instances of a core element (for example, multiple places of publication). For core elements, one instance of the element is required and subsequent instances are optional. For noncore elements, catalogers may include one, none, or some instances (Ehlert 2014, 4).

Access Points (0.7)

Using RDA, a cataloger can create authorized and variant access points to represent works, expressions, persons, families, or corporate bodies.

Authorized access points may also represent relationships. RDA offers guidelines for creating authorized access points for four types of relationship.

- The primary relationship between a manifestation and a work or expression embodied in it. (Note that these relationships are covered in section 5, chapter 17. LC has not implemented this section.)
- Relationships between a resource and persons, families, and corporate bodies associated with it. (Covered in section 6, chapters 18, 19–22. Data is entered in bibliographic records and sometimes in authority records. Uses Appendix I.)
- Relationships between works, expressions, manifestation, and items. (Covered in section 8, chapters 24, 25–28. Entered in bibliographic and/or authority records. Uses Appendix J.)
- Relationships between persons, families, and corporate bodies. (Covered in section 9, chapters 29, 30–32. Uses Appendix K. Data is entered in authority records.)

RDA also gives instructions on using various title elements (title proper, variant title, etc.) as access points.

Alternatives and Options (0.8) and Exceptions (0.9)

RDA frequently offers alternatives, optional instructions, and exceptions to rules.

An alternative is defined as providing "an alternative to what is specified in the immediately preceding guideline or instruction" (RDA, 0.8). A cataloger can choose to follow the rule or the alternative.

Optional instructions offer the opportunity to either supplement required data with additional information, or omit data from what is instructed in the preceding rule (RDA, 0.8). Here again, libraries can decide when or whether to follow the options or stick with the rule.

Exceptions must be followed when applicable. They are provided when it's necessary to depart from a rule's instructions because of a specific type of resource or situation (RDA, 0.9). (See Alternatives, Options, and Exceptions in RDA)

Examples (0.10) and Encoding RDA Data (0.12)

When working with RDA, it's important to keep in mind that it is a content standard. As such, it doesn't deal with presentation of data in its main rules. RDA prescribes what data to include in resource and entity descriptions, but it does not tell you how to format or punctuate it, what encoding scheme to use, or how to present or display it. The schema-neutral approach impacts your use of RDA in several ways, most particularly,

- In the kinds of examples RDA provides (0.10)
- In the need to map RDA into MARC and to consult appendices for information on punctuation (0.12)

Alternatives, Options, and Exceptions in RDA (RDA 0.8 and 0.9)

Alternative	An alternative to what is specified in the immediately preceding guideline or instruction.	Cataloger's choice whether to follow rule or its alternative.
Option		
Optional Addition	The optional addition of data that supplement what is called for in the immediately preceding instruction.	Cataloger's choice whether to add optional data.
Optional Omission	The optional omission of specific data called for in the immediately preceding instruction.	Cataloger's choice whether to omit data.
Exception	Takes precedence over the immediately preceding instruction and applies to a specific type of resource, condition, etc.	Cataloger must follow exception when applicable.

Examples (0.10)

In RDA, most of the examples illustrate only the specific rule under consideration. They generally lack punctuation or references to preceding elements. In the current cataloging environment, where libraries encode in MARC and follow ISBD (International Standard Book Description), some catalogers find the examples vague and lacking in context.

To illustrate, compare an example of the same statement of responsibility example as it appears in AACR2 and RDA:

AACR2 (5.1F1.)
La vie parisienne [GMD] : operetta in three acts / Jacques Offenbach ; music adapted and arranged by Ronald Hanmer ; new book and lyrics by Phil Park

RDA (2.4.2.3)
Jacques Offenbach
music adapted and arranged by Ronald Hanmer
new book and lyrics by Phil Park

The AACR2 example offers visual clues and context, placing the statement of responsibility after the title and preceded by a "/" (forward slash). It's easy to place the AACR2 example as belonging in a 245 MARC title field. In contrast, the RDA example floats in space, giving data in three separate lines, and offering few clues as to how to punctuate or where to place the information in the bibliographic record.

Encoding RDA Data (0.12 and Appendices D and E)

To assist with implementing the new cataloging code, RDA includes appendices on how to use it with the ISBD specification and MARC 21 encoding scheme. Appendix D.1 describes RDA using ISBD. Appendix D.2 directs you to the Tools area of RDA to access the RDA to MARC bibliographic mapping. Appendix E.1 provides information on punctuating access points in RDA. Appendix E.2 points to the Tools area for authority record mapping.

The maps for bibliographic and authority data are freely available from the "Tools" tab under RDA mapping, accessed via the RDA access URL (http://access.rdatoolkit.org/). They can be extremely useful as a roadmap from RDA to MARC. There are also maps in the other direction, from MARC to RDA. If you ever wonder what happened to a certain field under RDA, or where in RDA a certain MARC element is covered, the MARC to RDA maps can help answer your question.

Navigating RDA

NAVIGATING RDA—AN EXAMPLE

One of the more challenging aspects of learning RDA is that you often need to follow a path through multiple rules, rather than consult just one, to determine what you are expected to do. This seems to be a built-in characteristic of RDA's organization. It moves from general to specific and finally gets to actual instructions on how to record data at the end of chapters. Even then, at the point of instruction, it often sends you back to previous parts of the chapter, to different chapters, to appendices, to LC-PCC (Library of Congress–Program for Cooperative Cataloging) Policy Statements, or to all four.

If you are likely to be consulting RDA's text for answers, you should expect a learning curve to get used to navigating within it. For those using the *Toolkit,* the tree-structure table of contents can be very useful. Others may prefer to access rules via the index. Still others will go to the RDA Quick Search box. Another approach if you are using the *Toolkit* is to start in AACR2 and locate the rule you know in it. From there, you can link into the corresponding RDA rule. Whichever approach makes most sense to you is the one to go with, or keep them all in your own toolkit.

- Navigating RDA in the *RDA Toolkit:*
  - Use the tree-structure table of contents.
  - Use the index.
  - Use the RDA Quick Search box.
  - Begin in AACR2 at a known rule. Link into the corresponding RDA rule.

One reason for RDA's apparent redundancy is that information is divided up and parceled out at different levels of specificity. For example, some rules are entered at the general element level because they apply at that level. Rules that apply only to a more specific situation or subelement are supplied further down in the hierarchy. We see this in action for rules on recording titles and edition statements in chapter 2. Another reason is that attributes are often defined in the early part of a chapter and then instructions on how to record or use the attributes to create access points come later in the chapter. This is evident in chapter 6 on identifying works and expressions.

Example—Recording Title Proper

If you were looking for the rules on how to record title proper, you would find that the table of contents offers several places to start. You have a choice to drill down from the general concept element, Title, or work your way up from the specific element, Title Proper, which will actually be recorded.

Drill Down or Work Up

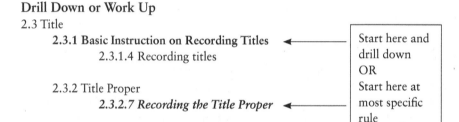

2.3 Title

2.3.1 Basic Instruction on Recording Titles ◄————— Start here and drill down OR

    2.3.1.4 Recording titles

2.3.2 Title Proper

    2.3.2.7 Recording the Title Proper ◄————— Start here at most specific rule

I prefer to work bottom up and start at the specific rule. In this manner, I know that I will encounter the fullest set of alternatives, options, exceptions, LC-PCC Policy Statements, and appendices. In this example, I would start at rule 2.3.2.7, Recording the Title Proper. Rule 2.3.2.7 reads,

> Record the title proper by applying the basic instructions at 2.3.1.

Rule 2.3.2.7 also features a list of examples, and an instruction to "Record an alternative title as part of the title proper." An LC-PCC Policy Statement offers instructions on nonfiling characters and what to do when a monographic series or multipart monograph lacks a title. Depending on what you are cataloging, these instructions and examples could prove important.

Moving up the chain to rule 2.3.1, Basic Instructions on Recording Titles, you find:

- 2.3.1.1 Scope
- 2.3.1.2 Sources of Information
- 2.3.1.3 Facsimiles and Reproductions
- 2.3.1.4 Recording Titles
  - o "Transcribe a title as it appears on the source of information (see 1.7)"

You are given an instruction here, but you are also advised to consult a more general rule. Before you go, note the optional omission for abridging titles and the exceptions for introductory words and inaccuracies for serials and integrating resources. These rules might apply to your particular situation.

At 1.7, Transcription, you will find instructions on:

- 1.7.2 Capitalization
- 1.7.3 Punctuation
- 1.7.4 Diacritical marks
- 1.7.5 Symbols
- 1.7.6 Spacing of initials and acronyms
- 1.7.7 Letters or words intended to be read more than once
- 1.7.8 Abbreviations
- 1.7.9 Inaccuracies

To find out how to capitalize for a title proper, you would consult 1.7.2.

At 1.7.2, Capitalization, you are told, "Apply the instructions on capitalization in appendix A."

At Appendix A, Capitalization, you find A.1, General Guideline, where you see an alternative that allows cataloging agencies

> to establish in-house guidelines for capitalization or to choose a published style manual, etc., as its preferred guide (see the alternative at 1.10.2). When this occurs, use those guidelines or that style manual instead of appendix A.

And there is an LC-PCC Policy Statement about the alternative, encouraging, but not requiring, LC catalogers to follow Appendix A.

> LC practice/PCC practice for Alternative: For capitalization of transcribed elements, catalogers are encouraged (but not required) to follow Appendix A; it is permitted to "take what you see" on the resource.

Keeping the alternative in mind, scroll down to A.3, Titles of Works, and A.3.1, General Guidelines, where you are instructed,

> Capitalize the title of a work as instructed at A.4.

At A.4, Titles of Manifestations, you will find A.4.1, General Guidelines, which states:

> Capitalize the first word or the abbreviation of the first word in a title, or in a title of a part, section, or supplement (see 2.3.1.7). Capitalize other words within titles by applying the guidelines at A.10–A.55, as applicable to the language involved.

Here, at A.4.1, is the instruction on capitalization for a title proper. However, you have been given some options along the way. You can follow the instruction at A.4, taking LC-PCC's advice, and transcribe the title the way you did in AACR2, capitalizing only the first word or abbreviation. Or you may follow the alternative at A.1 and transcribe the title proper as your agency has decided. One option is to choose to transcribe titles exactly as seen on a resource—hence the possibility of recording a title in all capitals, or with the first letter of every word capitalized. Other options are to follow a specific style guide, or to establish your own guidelines.

To complete your work on recording the title proper, you might have to consult rules about punctuation, diacritics, or errors in the title proper. To do so, you would need to consult other appropriate sections of 1.7.

There are many examples of RDA's apparently repetitive, drill-down structure. A simple perusal of the table of contents will reveal them. The more often you encounter the structure, the clearer it becomes. You will build a familiarity with it and find that you are successfully navigating RDA.

8

Tips for Using RDA

This chapter reviews additional features of RDA that can be helpful in learning to navigate through the content standard.

SCOPE, TERMINOLOGY, OBJECTIVES AND PRINCIPLES, CORE ELEMENTS

Each of RDA's ten sections has a general guidelines chapter that offers basic information on the section's contents, including its scope, terminology, and core elements.

Scope

The statements on scope in the general guidelines identify which RDA FRBR-FRAD entities the section deals with. If you are looking for information on a specific topic, the scope statements can help you decide whether you are in the right place. Subsequent chapters in each section offer more detailed purpose and scope information and can also help you to locate desired information.

For example, the scope statement in chapter 1 is quite general, stating that the section covers the attributes for two RDA entities—manifestations and items. In chapter 3, the scope statement more specifically describes the manifestation attributes of carrier information.

RDA 1.0 Scope
This chapter provides background information to support the application of guidelines and instructions in chapters 2–4 on recording attributes of manifestations and items.

RDA 3.0 Purpose and Scope
This chapter provides general guidelines and instructions on recording the attributes of the carrier of the resource. These attributes or characteristics are recorded using the elements covered in this chapter.

The elements in chapter 3 are typically used to select a resource that meets the user's needs in terms of:
   a) the physical characteristics of the carrier
   b) the formatting and encoding of the information contained in or stored on the carrier.

Terminology

RDA uses terms in very specific ways, and you need to stay aware of exactly what the RDA instructions are discussing. To help with this, the general guidelines chapters provide definitions for the terms and concepts addressed in their sections. For example, chapter 8, the general guidelines chapter for Section 3: Recording Attributes of Person, Family, & Corporate Body, provides definitions for "person," "family," "corporate body," "name," and "access point."

Core Elements

The general guidelines also list the core elements used in the following chapters of its section. The list is in hierarchical format; the main element (category) is given and then core subelements are indented. (RDA, 1.3)

- Title
  o Title proper
- Edition statement
  o Designation of edition

Core elements are also identified within the specific chapters where they are discussed. Hence, at RDA 2.3, Title, you find the main element (title) identified as core.

2.3 Title
CORE ELEMENT
The title proper is a core element. Other titles are optional.

And further down, at 2.3.2, you'll see title proper, the subelement, marked as core.

2.3.2 Title Proper
CORE ELEMENT

An element may also be "core if . . ." meaning that the element is required "if" a specific situation arises. For example, a copyright date is "core if" no date of publication or distribution can be provided (RDA, 2.11).

2.11 Copyright Date
CORE ELEMENT
Copyright date is a core element *if* neither the date of publication nor the date of distribution is identified.

The Library of Congress has identified additional core elements that it requires for its own cataloging. They are referred to as "LC core" elements. A full list of combined RDA and LC core elements is available from the Library of Congress website at http://www.loc.gov/aba/rda/pdf/core_elements.pdf.

SOURCES OF INFORMATION

In a change from AACR2, the chief source of information has become the preferred source of information in RDA. Preferred sources of information are defined in chapter 2 for resources consisting of pages, leaves, sheets, or cards (2.2.2.2), moving images (2.2.2.3), and other resources (2.2.2.4). They are used with the elements recorded in chapter 2, such as the title proper. Elsewhere, RDA defines "sources of information," sometimes providing a prioritized list and sometimes specifying "any source." When information is supplied from outside the resource, it is generally recorded in square brackets (Library of Congress, "RDA: Module 1," 11).

Within RDA's contents, sources of information follow a pattern and appear at _1.1 or at _.1.1.2. The exception to this is chapter 2, where sources are discussed at 2.2.

- Section 1: Chapters 2.2, 3.1.1, 4.1.1
- Section 2: Chapters 6.1.1, 7.1.1
- Section 3: Chapters 9.1.1, 10.1.1, 11.1.1
- Section 6: Chapters 19.1.1, 20.1.1, 21.1.1, 22.1.1
- Section 8: 25.1.1.2, 26.1.1.2, 27.1.1.2, 28.1.1.2
- Section 9: 30.1.1.2, 31.1.1.2, 32.1.1.2

LC-PCC POLICY STATEMENTS

We encountered LC-PCC Policy Statements (LC-PCC PS) in our navigating example in chapter 7. Policy statements are issued in places where the Library of Congress (LC) or the Program for Cooperative Cataloging (PCC) specify their policy and practice decisions regarding an RDA rule.

The policy statements are incorporated into the *RDA Toolkit*, so that at any point where an opinion has been issued, there is a green LC-PCC PS link to take you directly to it.

For those who don't have *Toolkit* subscriptions, the LC-PCC Policy Statements are available from the "free" portion of the *Toolkit* website. From the access URL (http://access.rdatoolkit.org/) click on the Resources tab and select Library of Congress–Program for Cooperative Cataloging Policy Statements (LC-PCC PS).

Many libraries follow LC's policies as a matter of course, and for these institutions it will be important to know what LC-PCC has decided to do. Other libraries use the LC-PCC statements as input when they are deciding for themselves how they want to apply a specific rule, option, or alternative in RDA.

As an example, there is an LC-PCC Policy Statement regarding the optional omission to abridge a long title mentioned above.

2.3.1.4 Recording Titles
Transcribe a title as it appears on the source of information (see 1.7).

Optional Omission
Abridge a long title only if it can be abridged without loss of essential information. Use a mark of omission (. . .) to indicate such an omission. Never omit any of the first five words.

LC-PCC PS for 2.3.1.4 OPTION
LC practice/PCC practice for Optional omission: Generally do not abridge a title proper.

PRINCIPLE OF REPRESENTATION

As discussed earlier, RDA is a principles-based set of cataloging rules. If you are familiar with the principles, you may see them at work as you move through the rules.

The principle of representation plays a particularly important role in the way RDA's rules are implemented. In RDA, rule 0.4.3.4, the principle states that:

The data describing a resource should reflect the resource's representation of itself.

Working from this principle, the following impacts in RDA are evident:

A. A general approach of "take what you see and accept what you get."
B. More flexibility on issues of capitalization.
C. Fewer abbreviations (e.g., in edition statements).
D. Titles are not abridged.
E. Statements of responsibility and access points are not limited as in AACR2 (no more Rule of Three).

F. Errors are recorded as they appear, with notes or added titles to correct or explain them.

In LC's internal training, catalogers are told to follow a general guideline of "take what you see and accept what you get" (Library of Congress, "RDA: Module 1," 13). RDA generally follows this approach, either by incorporating it into its rules or by offering alternatives and options to do so. LC-PCC's policy decisions also lean toward its support.

RDA's "general guidelines on transcription" (1.7.1–9) provide instructions for capitalization, punctuation, abbreviations, and inaccuracies (among others). But at 1.7.1, an alternative is provided to allow an agency to establish its own policies about these things. Thus, individual library agencies have an option to follow RDA, establish their own policies, or perhaps follow a published style manual.

In the case of capitalization, LC-PCC's policy statement (1.7.1, First Alternative) encourages following rules for capitalization, but permits catalogers to take what they see. Hence, when transcribing a title, libraries can choose to follow RDA's capitalization guidelines (capitalize the first word only) or transcribe exactly what appears on the preferred source of information.

For editions, RDA's rules support the "take what you see" approach. Rule 2.5.1.4 states, "Transcribe an edition statement as it appears on the source of information (see 1.7)." Upon consulting 1.7.8, you will be directed to Appendix B, Abbreviations. There you will find B.4, "For transcribed elements, use only those abbreviations found in the sources of information for the element." Here we see the "representation" principle impacting the use of abbreviations.

The principle is also at work when it comes to long titles or long statements of responsibility. At 2.3.1.4, RDA instructs us to "transcribe a title as it appears on the source of information." There is an optional omission to abridge a title, but LC-PCC's policy statement advises, "Generally do not abridge a title proper."

Similarly, at 2.4.1.5, Statement Naming More Than One Person, Etc. [in a statement of responsibility], the RDA instruction is to include all named entities. In the case of more than three, the optional omission allows you to "omit any but the first of each group of such persons, families, or bodies." The LC-PCC policy on the omission is, "Generally do not omit names in a statement of responsibility."

A final example of the principle of representation at work is RDA's approach to errors in transcribed elements. Rule 1.7.9 states,

1.7.9 Inaccuracies
When instructed to transcribe an element as it appears on the source, transcribe an inaccuracy or a misspelled word unless the instructions for a specific element indicate otherwise (e.g., exception at 2.3.1.4).

This means that when recording a title proper, catalogers will transcribe any error(s) found in the preferred source of information, using a "take what you see" approach. A note or added title can be used to correct the error.

Although there are many places in RDA where "take what you see" is implemented, there are also places where it is not. Careful observance of whether RDA says to "record" or "transcribe" can sometimes clarify the situation.

RECORD AND TRANSCRIBE

RDA uses the verbs "record" and "transcribe" with very specific meanings. "Record" is the general term that RDA uses to indicate that data should be put down, written, or entered (in a record) to describe a resource. "Transcribing" is a specific way to record data. In RDA it generally means to take what you see and copy it as is (Library of Congress, "RDA: Module 1," 13). When RDA uses "record" in specific instructions it indicates that you might be altering or adjusting data found in the preferred source of information. You might also be supplying or choosing data (as in choosing a preferred title).

You can see the various uses of "record" and "transcribe" by comparing the instructions for edition statement and extent of text. For editions, the heading for the instruction reads "Recording Edition Statements." RDA uses the term in its general application here, that is, edition data should be put into the bibliographic record. The actual instruction, however, calls for "transcribing" as the proper way to put down the data, "*Transcribe* an edition statement as it appears on the source of information" (RDA 2.5.1.4).

Instructions for extent of text also show the heading "Recording Extent." But here, the specific rule states, "*Record* the extent of the resource by giving the number of units and the type of unit" (RDA 3.4.1.3). When entering the extent of a resource, you are supplying data that you can take from several sources and thus are not explicitly copying (transcribing) exactly what you see (RDA 3.4.1.2).

NOT IN MARC OR AACR2 ORDER

Finally, it's worth observing here that RDA rules do not follow the current "normal" path for cataloging. AACR2 was purposefully written to "follow the sequence of catalogers' operations in most present-day libraries and bibliographic agencies" (AACR2 0.3). RDA is not. It looks toward the future and is correlated with FRBR and FRAD models, not with the order of elements on a standard catalog card. As a result, when cataloging with RDA in the MARC/ISBD environment, one jumps around between chapters a bit more than one did in AACR2. Its sequence of rules does not follow the sequence of elements we are used to. (See AACR2 "Cataloging Order" versus RDA Order)

AACR2 "Cataloging Order" versus RDA Order

Order of Elements on a Catalog Card	AACR2 Rule	Corresponding Elements in RDA	RDA Rule	Corresponding MARC Field
Title/Statement of Responsibility Area	1.1	Title	2.3	245 subfield 'a'
		Statement of Responsibility	2.4	245 subfield 'c'
Edition Area	1.2	Edition Statement	2.5	250
Publication, Distribution, etc. Area	1.4	Production Statement	2.7	260 (AACR2) 264 (RDA)
		Publication Statement	2.8	264
		Distribution Statement	2.9	264
		Manufacture Statement	2.10	264
		Copyright Date	2.11	264 $c
Physical Description Area	1.5	—		300 abc (AACR2)
		Describing Carrier—Extent	3.4	300 a (RDA)
		Describing Carrier—Dimension	3.5	300 c (RDA)
		Describing Content	7.15 7.17 7.18 7.22	300 b (RDA) 7.22 in 300 a
Series Area	1.6	Series Statement	2.12	4xx/8xx
Notes	1.7	Note on Manifestation/ Note on Item	2.17 2.21	5xx
Standard Number and Terms of Availability Area	1.8	—		02X
		Identifier for the Manifestation	2.15	02X
		Terms of Availability	4.2	02X (and other)

RDA also takes a different approach to classes of materials. In RDA, rules for specific formats follow general rules in the same chapter. In AACR2, rules for specific formats are given in separate chapters. For example, in AACR2, the rule for a devised title is found in chapter 1 (1.1B7). The rule for devised *music* titles is given in chapter 5 (5.1B2). In RDA, general rules for devised titles are found at 2.3.2.11, and rules for devised music titles follow in the same chapter at 2.3.2.11.1.

CONCLUSION

The past several chapters looked closely at general characteristics of RDA's text. We identified guideposts for navigating within it and looked at the challenges involved in using it. With this awareness, we are ready to move on to using RDA to catalog in MARC.

Part Two

RDA Into Marc

9

The "RDA into MARC" Workflow: An Overview

Having reviewed the basic structural characteristics of RDA's text, we turn now to using it in a MARC environment. It's a bit like fitting a square peg into a round hole.

RDA INTO MARC: A NEW WORKFLOW

RDA introduces a new conceptual approach to cataloging. At a simple level, we can say that RDA is not in MARC order, but in truth the change goes far deeper than that. It rests in the conceptual changes that FRBR and FRAD introduce to the cataloging process, and the resulting changes in how we think about and what we call things. This is the more challenging, and important, part of RDA.

Using RDA, the process for creating a bibliographic description follows the general workflow outlined below. In some places, especially in describing manifestations, the process feels similar to AACR2. It's the steps and parts that are not covered in the same order or in the same way that can be challenging to figure out. (See also RDA into MARC in Chapter 17)

Record Attributes of Manifestation and Item
Step 1. Identify the Manifestation and Item
- RDA section 1: chapter 2
- MARC 245, 246, 3xx, 4xx, 5xx

Step 2. Describe Carrier Elements
- RDA section 1: chapter 3
- MARC 337, 338, and 300a, 300c

Step 3. Provide Acquisitions and Access Information
- RDA section 1: chapter 4
- MARC 02x, 856

Record Attributes of Work and Expression
Step 4. Identify the Work and Expression/Assign Content Type
- RDA section 2: chapter 6
- MARC 100/110/111, 130, 240, (245), 7xx, 8xx
- MARC 336 (Content Type)

Step 5. Describe Content
- RDA section 2: chapter 7
- MARC 300a, 300b, 5xx

Identify Relationships
Step 6: Record the Relationships of the Resource to Persons, Families, or Corporate Bodies
- RDA section 6: chapters 18–22
- MARC 100, 110, 111, 700, 710, 711

Step 7: Record the Relationships of the Resource to Other Resources
- RDA section 8: chapters 24–28
- MARC 5xx, 7xx, (8xx, 490)

PARTS OF RDA NOT DIRECTLY USED FOR BIBLIOGRAPHIC DESCRIPTION

You may notice that not all of RDA's sections are cited in the process. There are several reasons for this. First, several of RDA's sections deal mostly with authority work and are not directly involved in the bibliographic description. These sections are nonetheless referred to and used in the process. Second, section 5 is not being used in RDA's initial implementation. Third, several sections have not yet been written.

Authority Sections
- Section 3: Recording Attributes of Persons, Families, and Corporate Bodies
  - Chapters 8–11 deal with the attributes used to create access points for persons, families, and corporate bodies.
  - Much of the data is recorded in authority records.
  - The access points created using the guidelines may be entered in bibliographic records.

- Section 9: Recording Relationships between Persons, Families, and Corporate Bodies
  - o These chapters (29–32) provide guidelines on expressing relations between persons, families, and corporate bodies, which are mostly recorded within the authority reference structure.

Not Applied
- Section 5: Recording Primary Relationships between Work, Expression, Manifestation, and Item
  - o This section (chapter 17) is not being applied in LC's initial implementation of RDA.

Not Written
- Section 4: Recording Attributes of Concepts, Objects, Events, and Places
  - o Chapters 12, 13, 14, 15 are not yet written. They will deal with creating access points for subjects (concepts, objects, events).
  - o Chapter 16, Places, does exist and deals with creating access points for places.
- Section 7: Recording Relationships to Concepts, Objects, Events, and Places
  - o Chapter 23 is not yet written. It will cover the relationships between a work and its subjects.
- Section 10: Recording Relationships between Concepts, Objects, Events, and Places
  - o Chapters 33–37 have not been written. They will cover relationships between subject entities and likely will be recorded as authority references.

RDA: REVIEW OF ITS TEN SECTIONS

In the following chapters we will review RDA section by section, focusing on the bibliographic description and the following goals:
- Become familiar with an RDA-based workflow.
- Identify RDA core, LC core, and LC/PCC core elements.
- Flag LC-PCC policy statements.
- Connect RDA contents with MARC and AACR2 practices:
  - o Note changes in rules and practice from AACR2.
  - o Specify new MARC fields and changes.
  - o Locate cataloging practices within RDA's text.

10

RDA Section 1:
Manifestations and Items

This chapter looks at the first three steps of the RDA into MARC workflow and covers RDA section 1.

Record Attributes of Manifestation and Item

Step 1. Identify the Manifestation and Item

- RDA section 1: chapter 2
- MARC 245, 246, 3xx, 4xx, 5xx

Step 2. Describe Carrier Elements

- RDA section 1: chapter 3
- MARC 337, 338, and 300a, 300c

Step 3. Provide Acquisitions and Access Information

- RDA section 1: chapter 4
- MARC 02x, 856

RDA Markers

Look for these symbols as you move through the text:

☐   Identifies RDA core, LC core, and PCC core elements ☐

✪   Starred LC-PCC policy statements ✪

Δ   Notes changes in rules and practice from AACR2 Δ

✚   Marks new MARC fields or changes in practice ✚

⊙   Targets/Locates cataloging practices within RDA's text ⊙

SECTION 1

Recording Attributes of Manifestation and Item

Section 1: Recording Attributes of Manifestation and Item	
Chapter	Title
1	General Guidelines on Recording Attributes of Manifestations and Items
2	Identifying Manifestations and Items
3	Describing Carriers
4	Providing Acquisition and Access Information

Section 1, Recording Attributes of Manifestation & Item, contains four chapters that together cover most of the elements used in creating a bibliographic description of a resource.

Chapter 1

Chapter 1 gives general guidelines for applying the rules in chapters 2 through 4 to describe manifestations and items.

1.4 Language and Script

RDA instructs catalogers to record many elements (listed in the section) in the language and script in which they appear on the resource. However, a first alternative says that if an element can't be recorded in the script, it should be transliterated.

✪ LC-PCC PS specifies that LC catalogers should Romanize data appearing in the fields listed at 1.4. Parallel (MARC 880) fields may be used to record the non-Roman data.

1.7 *Transcription*

Δ In a departure from AACR2 practice, RDA leans heavily toward "take what you see, accept what you get" when it comes to transcribed elements. Even so, there are guidelines as to capitalization, punctuation, abbreviations, inaccuracies, and so on, to cover recorded, supplied, and sometimes transcribed data. This section covers those.

Note the first alternative that gives libraries the option to set their own transcription policies or to follow a selected style manual. However,

✪ LC-PCC PS at Alternative 1: LC/PCC catalogers are encouraged to follow Appendix A on capitalization but may "take what they see."

1.11 *Facsimiles and Reproductions*

Δ RDA follows AACR2's practice of recording information about a facsimile in the body of the bibliographic description. Data about the original is recorded as a related manifestation (in a note). LC did not follow this guideline in AACR2, but is doing so with RDA. (The Program for Cooperative Cataloging [PCC] has raised issues with RDA's treatment of reproductions.)

Chapter 2

Chapter 2 offers guidelines for recording many common bibliographic attributes of resources.

- 2.3 Title
- 2.4 Statement of responsibility
- 2.5 Edition statement
- 2.6 Numbering of serials
- 2.7–2.11 Production, Publication, Distribution, Manufacture statements, and Copyright date
- 2.12 Series statement
- 2.13 Mode of issuance
- 2.14 Frequency
- 2.15 Identifier for the Manifestation
- 2.16 Preferred Citation
- 2.17 Note on Manifestation
- 2.18–2.20 Additional Attributes of Items
- 2.21 Note on Item

2.3. *Title*

☐ 2.3.2 Title proper is a core element, with specific instructions for the element beginning at 2.3.2. General information on Title is offered in section 2.3.1.

Δ Errors or typos in a title proper should be recorded as they appear (see 2.3.2.7, 2.3.1.4 [examples], and 1.7.9). This is a change from AACR2 practice.

Δ Transcribe an ellipsis (. . .) as it appears on the preferred source (1.7.3 examples).

Title proper is entered in MARC 245 subfield 'a'.

2.3.3 Parallel Title Proper

☐ ✪ LC-PCC PS: Parallel title proper is LC/PCC Core. Parallel title proper is a title proper in another language or script.

2.3.4 Other Title Information

☐ ✪ LC-PCC PS: Other title information (i.e., subtitle) is LC Core.

Other title information is entered in MARC 245 subfield 'b'.

2.3.6 Variant Title

✪ LC-PCC PS 2.3.6.3: Variant titles for a manifestation are recorded in MARC 246. Variant titles for a component of an aggregate work, where the authorized access point for the component will differ, may be recorded in MARC 740.

2.4 Statement of Responsibility

☐ The first statement of responsibility pertaining to the title proper is core.

Δ ☐ RDA's elimination of AACR2's Rule of Three means that catalogers may transcribe all entities listed as creators of, or contributors to, the content. Only the first named is required. See 2.4.1.4, Optional Omission and 2.4.2. LC and PCC generally record all entities (LC-PCC PS 2.4.1.4).

Δ Transcription of data means that terms such as "Jr." or "Dr." are recorded as they appear.

The statement of responsibility is recorded in MARC 245 subfield 'c'.

2.5 Edition Statement

☐ Designation of edition and designation of a named revision are core elements.

Δ Designation of edition is a transcribed element and should be taken from the resource as it appears. Do not use "ed." or other abbreviations unless they appear on the source (2.5.1.4).

Edition statements are transcribed in MARC 250 fields.

2.6 Numbering of Serials

☐ Core elements for this area are the first and last alpha/numeric and chronological designations for the serial. You are required to record the start and end points for a serial.

Numbering for serials may appear in the MARC 362, 363 fields.

2.7–2.11 Production, Publication, Distribution, and Manufacture Statements, and Copyright Date

Δ RDA provides separate elements for each of these entities. MARC provides the new field 264 to accommodate them.

2.7—Production Statement: Place, Name, Date (for nonpublished resources)

- ☐ Core if resource is unpublished
- ✚ MARC 264, second indicator '0', subfields $a, b, c

2.8—Publication Statement: Place, Name, Date

- ☐ Core for a published resource, if available
- ✚ MARC 264, second indicator '1', subfields $a, b, c

2.9—Distribution Statement

- ☐ Core if corresponding publication information is not available
- ✚ MARC 264, second indicator '2', subfields $a, b, c

2.10—Manufacture Statement

- ☐ Core if corresponding publication or distribution information is not available. For date, core if publication, distribution, or copyright date is unavailable
- ✚ MARC 264, second indicator '3', subfields $a, b, c

2.11—Copyright Date

- ☐ Core if date of publication or distribution is not available
- ✚ MARC 264, second indicator '4', subfield $c only

LC's policy statements and practices for these elements are further discussed in chapter 19 of the book.

2.12 Series Statement

☐ Title proper and numbering for the series and subseries are core.

❍ LC/PCC practice, in policy statement 2.12, is to transcribe a series for any comprehensive publication to which the resource being cataloged belongs. The policy statement provides detailed guidelines on entering series statements.

Series statement is recorded in the MARC 490 field.

2.13 Mode of Issuance

Δ This is a separate element in RDA. It is recorded as a code in the MARC leader position 07 bibliographic level. The 07 values are 'm' for a single unit or multipart monograph, 's' for a serial, and 'i' for an integrating resource.

The element is newly named in RDA, but the values for bibliographic level and MARC encoding are familiar.

2.15 Identifier for the Manifestation

☐ RDA Core. The identifier for a manifestation will most often be an ISBN, but may also include a music publisher or plate number. These are recorded in MARC 02x fields.

RDA instructs catalogers to include qualifiers when recording multiple identifiers (e.g., for a set and a part) or for an incorrect identifier. A new subfield 'q' has been defined for qualifying information in MARC 020, 024, 027, and 028.

2.17 Note on Manifestation

Guidelines for making notes on the elements defined in 2.3–2.14 are given in 2.17.2–2.17.12. A final note (2.17.13) deals with recording the issue, part, or iteration used as the basis for identifying a serial, multipart monograph, or integrating resource.

⊙ Many of AACR2's familiar notes are located here, specifically notes that pertain to the manifestation level of description.

❍☐ LC-PCC PS at 2.17 and 2.17.2 designate LC core status, when applicable, for notes on a title (2.17.2) in MARC 500.

❍☐ LC-PCC PS at 2.17 also designates LC core for notes on the issue, part, or iteration used as the basis for identification (RDA 2.17.13), entered in MARC 588 or 500.

Chapter 3

Chapter 3, Describing Carriers, introduces two of the three new elements that replace the GMD—media type and carrier type. Content type, the third element, is an expression-level element and is covered in RDA chapter 6.

See chapter 20 of this book for further information on media, carrier, and content type.

Δ 3.2 Media Type

✚ Enter media type in the new MARC 337 field.
❍☐ Media type is LC/PCC core, but not RDA core.

Δ 3.3 Carrier Type

✚ Enter carrier type in the new MARC 338 field.
☐ Carrier type is RDA core.

⊙ Parts of what AACR2 and MARC call the physical description are also covered in chapter 3.

3.4 *Extent*

Record Extent in the MARC 300 $a subfield.

□ RDA Core element, if resource is complete or if total extent is known.

Δ Spell out terms, for example, "pages," "volumes," "approximately," "that is" (not i.e.).

⊙ For information on recording duration, see 7.22 in RDA chapter 7, Describing Content.

After the basic instructions are given in 3.4.1, specific instructions for the following resources are provided:

- Cartographic resource (3.4.2)
- Notated music (3.4.3)
- Still image (3.4.4)
- Text (3.4.5)
- Three-dimensional form (3.4.6)

3.4.1.3 *Recording Extent: Use the list of carrier types at RDA 3.3.1.3 for naming units*

Δ "computer disc" is used for computer disk and computer optical disk.

Δ "audio disc" is used instead of "sound disc" for CDs.

An alternative at 3.4.1.3 gives libraries the option to use "a term in common usage" if preferred or if the carrier is not listed at 3.3.1.3. For example, some libraries opt to use CD or DVD for units of extent.

3.4.5.3 *Single Volumes with Unnumbered Pages, Leaves, or Columns*

Δ For pagination, use one of the options offered here rather than supplying estimated pages in square brackets.

✪ LC-PCC PS: Prefer option c: 1 volume (unpaged).

3.4.5.8 *Complicated or Irregular Paging, Etc.*

RDA provides three options for recording irregular paging.

✪ LC-PCC PS: Prefer option c: 1 volume (various pagings).

3.5 *Dimensions*

Record dimensions in the MARC 300 $c subfield.

□✪ LC-PCC PS: Dimensions is LC core, except for serials and online resources.

3.5.1.3 *Recording Dimensions*

Record dimensions in whole centimeters, rounding up.

Δ Use symbol 'cm' with no full stop (period).

If the 300$c field is followed by a 490 series field, then ISBD punctuation requires a full stop (period) at the end of 300$c. This effectively makes it look as if 'cm' is abbreviated (cm.).

3.5.1.3 Alternative

A library may use its preferred system of measurement.

❍ LC-PCC PS at 3.5.1.3 and 3.5.1.4.4 Alternative

LC practice: Use inches for discs and audio carriers. [Inches may be abbreviated (in.); see Appendix B.]

3.6–3.22

The remaining elements described in 3.6 to 3.22 cover a dizzying array of carrier characteristics for a variety of formats. Many of the elements are recorded in MARC 300 or 5xx notes.

✚ There are new MARC 34x fields where some of these elements may be recorded. Best practices for using the MARC 34x fields are still developing. In February 2014, the Music Library Association released its best practices for music cataloging with RDA, including its recommendations for use of the 34x fields (MLA 2014).

   ☐ ❍ 3.11 Layout—LC/PCC core for cartographic materials.
   ☐ ❍ 3.19 Digital File Characteristic—LC core for cartographic resources.
   ☐ ❍ 3.21 and 3.21.4 Note on Changes in Carrier Characteristics is LC core if carrier characteristics change and a new description is not made.

For additional information on how the elements in "Describing Carriers" are recorded for specific formats, see the RDA MARC examples in Part Three of the book.

Chapter 4

Elements in this chapter pertain to acquisitions and access information for the user. None of the elements are RDA core. Most of these elements are usually used for special collections, but the two below are also seen in general cataloging.

4.2.1.3 Recording Terms of Availability

⊙ RDA 4.2.1.3: If your library records price in the ISBN field (020 $c), guidelines are provided at 4.2.1.3.

❍ LC practice: In general, do not provide price or other terms of availability.

4.6 Uniform Resource Locator

☐❍ LC-PCC PS 4.6 : Uniform Resource Locator (URL) is LC Core when present. Catalogers record URLs in MARC bibliographic 856 fields.

✪ 4.6.1.3: LC-PCC PS: LC practice: Record all URLs that are provided in a resource.

CONCLUSION

In this chapter we followed steps 1 to 3 of the RDA into MARC cataloging process. We covered RDA section 1, chapters 1–4. These steps deal with describing manifestations (and to a much lesser extent items) and can feel very similar to the process in AACR2.

In the next chapter we will look at describing works and expressions.

11

RDA Section 2: Naming Works and Expressions

This chapter looks at the fourth step of the RDA into MARC workflow where we identify the work (and perhaps the expression) and assign a content type. We move to section 2 of RDA for our instructions.

Step 4. Identify the Work and Expression/Assign Content Type
- RDA section 2: chapter 6
- MARC 100/110/111, 130, 240, (245), 7xx, 8xx
- MARC 336 (Content Type)

RDA Markers

Look for these symbols as you move through the text:

☐　　　Identifies RDA core, LC core, and PCC core elements ☐

✪　　　Starred LC-PCC policy statements ✪

Δ　　　Notes changes in rules and practice from AACR2 Δ

✚　　　Marks new MARC fields or changes in practice ✚

⊙　　　Targets/Locates cataloging practices within RDA's text ⊙

SECTION 2: CHAPTERS 5–6

Recording Attributes of Work and Expression

Section 2: Recording Attributes of Work and Expression	
Chapter	Title
5	General Guidelines on Recording Attributes of Works and Expressions
6	Identifying Works and Expressions
7	Describing Content

RDA's section 2 deals with recording attributes of works and expressions. Some of its elements are recorded as bibliographic information, some as authority, and some as both. Chapter 5 provides general guidelines on attributes of works and expressions. Chapter 6 is concerned with choosing and recording preferred and variant titles for works and expressions and constructing authorized access points from them. It also covers content type (MARC 336), the third new element in the trio replacing the GMD.

Chapter 5

5.1 Terminology

5.1.3 Title: 'Title of the work' and 'Preferred title for the work' refer to the title by which a **work** is known, not the manifestation title that appears on the resource.

5.1.4 Access Points: 5.1.4 gives an overall description of how to construct the authorized access point representing a work or expression (see also 5.5, 5.6).

5.3 Core Elements

☐ The preferred title for a work is core when applicable and "readily ascertainable."

Content Type and Language of Expression are also core.

5.5 Authorized Access Points Representing Works and Expressions

☐ The authorized access point representing a work consists of the preferred title for the work preceded by the authorized access point for a creator, if applicable. Additional qualifiers are added as instructed at rule 6.27.1.9.

5.6 Variant Access Points Representing Works and Expressions

A variant access point representing a work or expression is comprised of the variant title for the work or expression, combined with the authorized access point for creator, if any. It is recorded as MARC authority data and would not appear in a bibliographic record.

5.7 Status of Identification, 5.8 Source Consulted, 5.9 Cataloger's Note

These three fields are recorded as MARC authority data.

Chapter 6

Δ In contrast to AACR2, RDA does away with the term Uniform Title and instead talks about the title of a work, its preferred title, and the authorized access point for the work or its expressions. Uniform titles are dealt with separately in AACR2 as part of the section on headings. RDA deals with them as part of identifying and describing works and expressions.

As we work our way through the chapter, bear in mind that for many resources a preferred title is not necessary. It is often the same as the title proper (which you have already recorded in chapter 2).

At 6.0, RDA suggests using authorized access points representing works and expressions for:

a) Bringing together all descriptions of resources embodying a work when various manifestations have appeared under various titles
b) Identifying a work when the title by which it is known differs from the title proper of the resource being described
c) Differentiating between works with the same title
d) Organizing hierarchical displays [of resources embodying expressions of a work]
e) Recording a relationship to a related work

The language used is similar to how AACR2 describes the uses of uniform titles in chapter 25, which include:

- Bringing together all catalog entries for a work when various manifestations (e.g., editions, translations) have appeared under various titles
- For identifying a work when the title by which it is known differs from the title proper of the item being catalogued

Chapter 6 covers the following main points:

- Choosing and recording preferred titles
- Recording variant titles
- Constructing authorized access points for works and expressions
- Constructing variant access points for works and expressions
- Recording other attributes of works and expressions (including Content Type, an expression-level attribute)

Organizationally, chapter 6 lists the attributes used to identify a work or an expression at the beginning. Work attributes are in 6.2–8. Expression attributes are listed from 6.9 to 6.13. Later in the chapter, at 6.27, instructions on constructing access points for works and expressions are provided. Section 6.27.1 tells us how to construct access points for works. Section 6.27.3 covers expressions.

Naming the Work—Identifying Works

6.2 Title of the Work (Naming the Work)

The process for identifying a work in RDA is akin to that followed for determining the main entry in AACR2. RDA (and LC in its training) refers to the process as naming the work and naming the expression (Library of Congress, "RDA: Module 2," 15). The data identified in the process can be recorded in the MARC bibliographic record in the following fields:

- 1xx + 240
- 1xx + 245
- 130 alone
- 240 alone

6.2.2 Preferred Title for the Work

To name the work, you choose (6.2.2.3) and record (6.2.2.8) the preferred title. For works after 1500, the preferred title is the form of title by which a work has become known (6.2.2.4).

□ The preferred title for a work is RDA core. (It may be represented by the title proper in MARC 245, or it may differ from the title proper and be recorded in the MARC 130 or 240 fields.)

Once you have decided on the preferred title, you determine whether there is a creator involved. If so, the creator is recorded with the preferred title to form the authorized access point.

⊙ The instruction to add a creator is found in the guidelines for constructing access points at 6.27, in the general guidelines at 5.5, and also in the introduction at 0.6.3.

□ Creator is a core element as specified at RDA 19.2. If there are more than one, only the principal creator or first-named is required.

6.2.3 Variant Title for the Work

Note that the element 'Variant Title for the Work' differs from the manifestation-level element 'Variant Title' (RDA 2.3.6). A variant title for a manifestation is recorded in the MARC 246 field. It is a title that appears elsewhere on a particular manifestation. The 'Variant Title for the Work' is a variation of a preferred title and would be entered in a MARC authority record as a reference.

6.3–6.6

Information should be added, if necessary, to make the preferred title unique and distinct within the catalog you are using.

☐ The following elements are RDA core if needed to differentiate the access point:

- Form of work (6.3)
- Date of work (6.4)
- Place of origin of the work (6.5)
- Other distinguishing characteristic of the work (6.6)

There is no priority for choosing which to use, and the distinguishing data can be taken from any source (6.3.1.2, 6.4.1.2, 6.5.1.2, 6.6.1.2). In bibliographic data, they are added in parentheses to the access point.

6.9–6.13

Rules 6.9 through 6.13 deal with attributes of expressions. We'll look at them later in this chapter.

6.14–6.26

Rules 6.14 through 6.26 discuss special considerations for musical, legal, or religious works. They are outside the scope of our discussion.

Right now we'll jump to 6.27.1 so that we can complete the process of naming the work.

6.27.1 [Constructing] Authorized Access Point Representing a Work

Section 6.27.1 provides directions on constructing access points for a variety of situations.

- 6.27.1.2 Works created by one creator
- 6.27.1.3 Collaborative works
- 6.27.1.4 Compilations of works by different creators
  - ○ See also 6.2.2.10 for compilations of one creator's works.
- 6.27.1.5 Adaptations and Revisions
- 6.27.1.6 Commentary, Annotations, Illustrative Content, Etc., Added to a Previously Existing Work
- 6.27.1.7 Different Identities for an Individual Responsible for a Work
- 6.27.1.8 Works of Uncertain or Unknown Origin

In addition, catalogers are directed to 6.28.1 for musical works, 6.29.1 for legal works, 6.30.1 for religious works, and 6.31.1 for official communications.

Δ RDA handles collaborations and compilations somewhat differently than AACR2. Further details are provided in chapter 21 of the book.

The instructions at 6.27.1 are used in conjunction with section 3, chapters 9, 10, and 11, as well as section 6, chapter 19, if identifying creators is involved in naming the work. Chapters 9–11 contain rules about the attributes used to identify persons, families, and corporate bodies (in that order). Chapter 19 offers guidelines on expressing the relationship of persons, corporate bodies, and families associated with a work.

Persons, families and corporate bodies can be creators in RDA.

Δ RDA distinguishes between creators and contributors:

Creator:
A person, family, or corporate body responsible for the *creation of a work*.

Contributor:
A person, family, or corporate body *contributing to an expression*. Contributors include editors, translators, arrangers of music, performers, etc.

Δ In a change from AACR2, a composer remains a creator, but a performer becomes a contributor. Illustrators are also considered contributors, as are editors and translators.

Δ If a compilation or a modification of a work results in a new work, then those responsible can also be considered creators.

Δ Fictitious or real nonhuman entities can be creators.

6.27.2 Part or Parts of a Work

Guidelines at 6.27.2, Authorized Access Point Representing a Part or Parts of a Work, along with its counterpart at 6.2.2.9, Recording the Preferred Title for a Part or Parts of a Work, provide details on how to handle works that contain one part, or multiple parts, of a larger work. Examples cited include Tolkien's *Lord of the Rings* and its parts, or Dante's *Divine Comedy*.

Identifying Expressions

Now back to expressions. Attributes for identifying expressions are listed at the beginning of chapter 6, beginning at 6.9. Instructions on constructing an authorized access point for an expression come at the end. The authorized access point for a work is the beginning point for constructing an authorized access point for an expression.

There are four elements for expressions described in 6.9–6.12.

6.9 Content Type

Content type is the third of three new RDA elements that are meant to replace the GMD. Its mates, media type and carrier type, are discussed in RDA chapter 3 as manifestation-level attributes. Chapter 20 of the book talks more about content, media and carrier types.

☐ Content type is RDA core.

✚ Enter content type in the new MARC 336 field.

6.10 Date of Expression

☐ RDA Core if needed to distinguish between expressions.

❂ LC-PCC PS 6.27.3: For authorized access points, LC uses date of expression for music, sacred scripture, and translations and language editions only.

Δ LC no longer requires the date of expression for compilations with the collective title "Works."

Record the date as a separate element or as part of an access point in the bibliographic or authority record. (MARC 045, 046 or as part of the heading in the bibliographic record; 046 or in 1xx, 4xx, 5xx fields in the authority record.)

6.11 Language of Expression

☐ RDA Core

❂ LC-PCC PS 6.11.1.3: Use the MARC Code List for Languages for recording the name of a language (http://www.loc.gov/marc/languages/).

In addition to being added to an authorized access point, language of expression may be recorded as a separate element in MARC at several places in the bibliographic record:

008/35-37 Language MARC code
546 Language note
✚ New MARC field 377

6.12 Other Distinguishing Characteristic of the Expression

☐ Core if needed to distinguish between expressions in an authorized access point.

✚ New MARC field 381 can also be used to record this information.

These four attributes (6.9–6.12) can be used as qualifiers to make an authorized access point for an expression unique. In practice, LC only uses them for very specific formats, as specified by the policy statement at 6.27.3. We'll go to 6.27.3 now to complete our discussion of identifying expressions by looking at LC practice for translations and language editions.

6.27.3 Authorized Access Point Representing an Expression

❂ LC-PCC PS 6.27.3: Identify expressions by adding an expression attribute to the authorized access point for the work in the following situations:

- Music resources
- Sacred scripture resources
- Translations
- Language editions

LC-PCC 6.27.3—Translations

When a work is translated into another language, different from its original language of expression, it becomes a new expression. To construct an authorized access point to represent the expression, the policy statement tells us to add the translation language to the authorized access point for the work. In MARC terms, we add the language in subfield 'l' in MARC x30, 240, 7xx, or 8xx.

Δ Do not use "Polyglot" or multiple languages connected with an ampersand (e.g., "French & Spanish") in subfield 'l'.

Examples

Authorized access point for the Spanish language translation/expression of *Curious George Flies a Kite*:

240: $a Curious George flies a kite. $l Spanish.

Authorized access points for the original language expression (no $l) and the translated language expression (include $l) for a work that contains both:

700: $a Dante Alighieri, $d 1265–1321. $t Divina commedia.
700: $a Dante Alighieri, $d 1265–1321. $t Divina commedia. $l English.
(Library of Congress, "RDA: Module 3," 5)

LC-PCC 6.27.3—Language Editions

The CONSER Cataloging Manual glossary defines "language edition" as:

A serial published simultaneously in different languages. The publisher of all of the editions is usually the same. The titles may be in different languages or in the same language.

Language editions for serials follow similar guidelines as translations. Under RDA, the original language is designated based on which expression is received by the agency first. Construct the authorized access point for the work (in the designated original language), and add $l for the translation language to create the expression's authorized access point. For example: the authorized access point for an English language edition/expression of a French magazine:

130: $a Religions & histoire. $l English.
245: $a Religion and history.

6.28–6.31

The remaining four sections of chapter 6 discuss constructing access points to represent works and expressions for specific situations:

6.28 Musical works and expressions
6.29 Legal works and expressions
6.30 Religious works and expressions
6.31 Official communications

CONCLUSION

This chapter looked at naming works, identifying expressions, and assigning content types. It covered step 4 of the RDA into MARC process. In this step, we decide if we need a separate preferred title, whether to record a creator(s) for our work, and we assign a content type. If necessary, we identify the expression. In the next chapter we move to step 5 and to RDA chapter 7, and we look at describing content for works and expressions.

12

Describing Content for Works and Expressions

In the last chapter we named the work, identified creators, specified content type, and recorded expression-level data. Now we move into RDA's chapter 7, Describing Content. It is the fifth step in our RDA into MARC workflow.

Step 5. Describe Content
- RDA section 2: chapter 7
- MARC 300a, 300b, 5xx

RDA Markers

Look for these symbols as you move through the text:

☐ Identifies RDA core, LC core, and PCC core elements ☐

✪ Starred LC-PCC policy statements ✪

Δ Notes changes in rules and practice from AACR2 Δ

✚ Marks new MARC fields or changes in practice ✚

⊙ Targets/Locates cataloging practices within RDA's text ⊙

SECTION 2: CHAPTER 7

Recording Attributes of Work and Expression

Section 2: Recording Attributes of Work and Expression	
Chapter	Title
5	General Guidelines on Recording Attributes of Works and Expressions
6	Identifying Works and Expressions
7	Describing Content

The content attributes in chapter 7 are divided into work- and expression-level elements. The first eight elements (7.2–7.9) are work-level, and the remaining elements (7.10–7.29) are expression-level.

☐ There are two RDA core elements, both for cartographic content:

- Horizontal scale (7.25.3)
- Vertical scale (7.25.4)

LC-PCC Policy Statements designate additional core elements for LC and PCC, as noted below. In addition, LC designates core elements for music and cartographic resources.

Four of the expression-level elements are recorded in the 300 field of the MARC record.

☐✪ 7.15 Illustrative Content
- LC core for children's materials
- MARC 300 $b

7.17 Color Content
- Not LC core
- U.S. agencies: Use U.S. spelling "color"
- MARC 300 $b

Δ When describing illustrative or color content, terms are spelled out.

7.18 Sound Content
- Not LC core
- MARC 300 $b

☐✪ 7.22 Duration
- LC core
- MARC 300 $a

✪ 7.22.1.4 LC-PCC PS: When giving time units for duration in 300 $a, use abbreviations found in appendix B (e.g., hr., min.).

Many of the LC or LC/PCC core elements will be familiar to you as AACR2 notes.

□✪ Intended Audience
- RDA 7.7
- Work attribute
- LC core for children's materials
- MARC 521, coded field MARC 008/position 22

□✪ Dissertation or Thesis Information
- RDA 7.9
- Work attribute
- LC/PCC core for theses/dissertations
- MARC 502 or 500, coded field MARC 008/position 24
- Δ ✚ LC-PCC PS 7.9.1.3: Do not use AACR2 punctuation for 502 notes. RDA introduces new subfields and format for RDA's elements.

□✪ Summarization of the Content
- RDA 7.10
- Expression attribute
- LC core for children's fiction materials
- MARC 520 or 856 (for URL links to summaries)

□✪ Language of the Content
- RDA 7.12
- Expression attribute
- LC/PCC core
- MARC 546
- Use MARC Code List for Languages for codes or names of languages: http://www.loc.gov/marc/languages/
- LC-PCC PS 7.12.1.3: "In addition to recording the language of the primary content, also supply the languages of other content (summaries, tables of contents, etc.) if it will assist identification and selection." The policy statement shows both the 546 Language Note field and the 041 coded language field used to record language.

□✪ Supplementary Content (Bibliographies and Indexes)
- RDA 7.16
- Expression attribute
- LC core for bibliographies and indexes
- ✪ LC-PCC PS 7.16.1.3 MARC 504 (bibliography or bibliography and index) or 500 (index only)

Other elements (and notes) that you may be looking for, but which are not LC or LC/PCC core, are also included in chapter 7.

✪ **Accessibility Content**
- RDA 7.14
- Sign language or closed captioning note
- MARC 546

Performer, Narrator, and/or Presenter
- RDA 7.23
- Participant or Performer Note, Performers/Narrator note
- MARC 511

Artistic and/or Technical Credit
- RDA 7.24
- Creation/Production credits note
- MARC 508

Award
- RDA 7.28
- Award note
- MARC 586

CONCLUSION

We have now completed steps 1 through 5 of the RDA into MARC work-flow and completed most of the bibliographic description. Our workflow turns to Part Two of RDA, Recording Relationships. In our next chapter, we look at relationships that are recorded in bibliographic records when RDA is expressed in MARC.

13

RDA Section 6: Relationships of a Resource to Persons, Families, or Corporate Bodies

We'll now move into Part Two of RDA and look at relationships. We'll focus on relationships that are recorded in the bibliographic record. This is the sixth step of our RDA into MARC workflow.

> **Step 6: Record the Relationships of the Resource to Persons, Families, or Corporate Bodies**
> - RDA section 6: chapters 18–22
> - MARC 100, 110, 111, 700, 710, 711

RDA Markers

Look for these symbols as you move through the text:

☐	Identifies RDA core, LC core, and PCC core elements ☐
✪	Starred LC-PCC policy statements ✪
Δ	Notes changes in rules and practice from AACR2 Δ
✚	Marks new MARC fields or changes in practice ✚
☉	Targets/Locates cataloging practices within RDA's text ☉

RELATIONSHIPS

In RDA, there are two basic parts to recording a relationship:

- Identifying the entities that are related in some way
- Specifying the type of relationship between the entities

Part Two of RDA tells us how to express the relationships for the entities we've identified in Part One.

There are six sections in RDA's Part Two, but only three have been implemented in the initial release of RDA.

- Section 6: Relationships between a resource and persons, families, or corporate bodies
- Section 8: Relationships between works, expressions, manifestations, and items
- Section 9: Relationships between persons, families, and corporate bodies

Sections 7 and 10 are not yet written, and LC is not applying section 5 in their initial implementation. We are looking at section 6 and section 8 in this chapter. They deal most directly with relationships recorded in the bibliographic record.

SECTION 6

Recording Relationships to Persons, Families, & Corporate Bodies

Section 6: Recording Relationships to Persons, Families, and Corporate Bodies	
Chapter	Title
18	General Guidelines on Recording Relationships to Persons, Families, and Corporate Bodies *Associated with a Resource*
19	Persons, Families, and Corporate Bodies *Associated with a Work*
20	Persons, Families, and Corporate Bodies *Associated with an Expression*
21	Persons, Families, and Corporate Bodies *Associated with a Manifestation*
22	Persons, Families, and Corporate Bodies *Associated with an Item*

Section 6 discusses how to record relationships of persons, families, or corporate bodies to a resource (a work, expression, manifestation, or item). After the general guidelines in chapter 18, chapters 19–22 cover relationships with a work (chapter 19), an expression (chapter 20), a manifestation (chapter 21), and an item (chapter 22).

The relationship between a person, family, or corporate body and a resource is expressed in MARC in 1xx and 7xx bibliographic fields, using relationship designators from Appendix I.

- 100, 110, 700, 710 + subfield 'e' [relationship designator]
- 111, 711 + subfield 'j' [relationship designator]

The PCC recommends using designators for all creators and for all additional access points (Program for Cooperative Cataloging 2013, [1]).

Chapter 18: General Guidelines

18.1 Terminology

"Resource" is used here as meaning any of the WEMI entities—a work, expression, manifestation, or item.

18.3 Core Elements

☐ The principal or first-named creator of a work is RDA core.

☐ If another person, family, or corporate body is necessary to construct the authorized access point for a work, that entity/relationship is RDA "core if."

✪ ☐ Note: RDA 20.2, LC-PCC PS. LC designates Illustrator (a contributor) as a core relationship for children's materials.

18.4 Recording Relationships to Persons, Families, and Corporate Bodies Associated with a Resource

Record these relationships with an identifier or an authorized access point (18.4.1). Provide an identifier (18.4.1.1) or an authorized access point (18.4.1.2) by applying the appropriate instructions in section 3, chapters 9–11 (identifying persons, families, and corporate bodies).

✪ LC-PCC PS 18.4.1.1: LC/PCC practice: In the initial RDA implementation, do not use identifiers alone to indicate a relationship.

18.5 Relationship Designator

Δ Relationship designators are new in RDA.

18.5.1.3: Use Appendix I to find the specific designators you should apply in chapters 19–22. Those chapters do not reference Appendix I themselves. Appendix I is divided into separate sections pertaining to works (chapter 19/Appendix I.2), expressions (chapter 20/Appendix I.3), manifestations (chapter 21/Appendix I.4), and items (chapter 22/Appendix I.5). Terms from Appendix I are used in bibliographic records and should not be applied to MARC authority records.

18.6 Note on Persons, Families, and Corporate Bodies Associated with a Resource

Catalogers are referred to chapters 2.17 or 5.9 if it is felt that a note is necessary to explain the relationship.

Chapter 19: Creator/Other Relationships (Works)

19.2 Creator

☐ The principal or first-named creator is core.

✪ The LC-PCC PS at 19.2 allows cataloger judgment on recording additional creators.

✪ 19.2.1.1.1 and LC-PCC PS 19.2.1.1.1 Corporate Bodies Considered to Be Creators:

⊙ This is where "entry under corporate body" is explained (parallels AACR2 21.1B).

19.3 Other Person, Family, or Corporate Body Associated with a Work

We have talked only about creators at the work level so far. Chapter 19 also covers "others" associated with a work. These are not the same as contributors, who participate at an expression-level of a resource.

☐ The element is RDA core if the access point for the other person, family, or corporate body is needed to construct the authorized access point for the work (see 6.27–6.31). If it is not necessary, record it if it is considered important for access (19.3.1.3).

19.3.1.1 Scope

Examples of others associated with a work include:

- Persons to whom correspondence is addressed
- Persons honored by a festschrift
- Directors
- Cinematographers
- Sponsoring bodies
- Production companies
- Institutions hosting an exhibition or event

To construct the access points for both creators (19.2) and others, (19.3), chapter 19 refers catalogers back to 18.4, where instruction 18.4.1.2 directs you to Section 3, chapters 9, 10, and 11. To specify the relationship of these entities to your resource, assign a relationship designator from Appendix I.

Appendix I.2: Relationship Designators . . . Associated with a Work

Assign a designator from the appropriate section of Appendix I.2.

- I.2.1 Creators: Creator terms include architect, author, choreographer, compiler, and photographer.
- I.2.2 Others: "Others" designators include consultant, addressee, director (film, radio, television), host institution, judge, issuing body, plaintiff, and production company.

Do not apply a relationship designator from I.2.1 to an entity with an "other" relationship. The term must come from I.2.2.

Chapter 20: Contributor Relationships (Expressions)

Chapter 20 discusses guidelines for recording contributors associated with an expression.

20.2 Contributor

❂ ☐ LC-PCC PS 20.2: LC practice: Contributor is core for illustrators of children's materials only. Recording additional illustrators (if any) is left to the cataloger's judgment.

❂ PCC practice: Record contributors if they are considered important for identification.

Similarly to chapter 19, RDA rule 20.2.1.3 refers catalogers back to 18.4 for instructions on access points. Instruction 18.4.1.2 directs you to Section 3, chapters 9, 10, and 11. To specify the relationship of these entities to your resource, assign a relationship designator from Appendix I.

Appendix I.3: Relationship Designators . . . Associated with an Expression

Assign a relationship designator from Appendix I.3.

• Appendix 1.3.1, "Relationship Designators for Contributors," has only one section. Contributor designators include abridger, editor, costume designer, art director, illustrator, performer, puppeteer, storyteller, translator, and transcriber.

Chapter 21: Manifestation Relationships: Producer, Publisher, Manufacturer, or Distributor

21.0 Scope

In addition to recording attributes for the separate elements of producer, publisher, distributor, or manufacturer (RDA chapter 2, MARC 264), you may also provide an access point for the relationship of these elements to the resource (in MARC 7xx) if it is considered important. The relationship occurs at the manifestation level. None of the relationships are core.

21.2 Producer of an Unpublished Resource*
21.3 Publisher
21.4 Distributor
21.5 Manufacturer (printing, duplicating, casting)
21.6 Others*

Catalogers are again referred back to 18.4, and thence to Section 3 for instructions on access points. To specify the relationship of these entities to your resource, assign a relationship designator from Appendix I.4.

---

* At the time of writing, there are no specific relationship designators for these entities in Appendix I.4.

Appendix I.4: Relationship Designators . . . Associated with a Manifestation

Assign a relationship designator from Appendix I.4 from the appropriate section:

- I.4.1 Manufacturers: Designators for manufacturers include book designer, engraver, and platemaker.
- I.4.2 Publishers: Broadcaster is the only relationship designator in Appendix I.4.2 at the time of this writing.
- I.4.3 Distributors: At the time of this writing, appendix I.4.3 contains only the term "film distributor" as a relationship designator.

Chapter 22: Item Relationships: Owners, Custodians, Others

Persons, families, and corporate bodies associated with an item are the subject of chapter 22. These relationships are recorded if the cataloger considers them important for access. None of them are core.

22.2 Owner
22.3 Custodian
22.4 Others

Here again you are sent back to RDA 18.4, and thence to Section 3 for instructions on access points. Relationship designators are assigned from Appendix I.

Appendix I.5: Relationship Designators . . . Associated with an Item

Assign a relationship designator from Appendix I.5:

- I.5.1 Owners: Owners can be current, or former. A depositor is a kind of current owner.
- I.5.2 Others: The "other" category includes annotator, binder, curator, or restorationist.

There are no relationship designators for Custodians (22.3) at the time of writing.

CONCLUSION

This chapter discussed how to record relationships between a resource and a person, family, or corporate body. We looked at creators, others associated with a resource, and contributors. This information is covered in section 6 of RDA. Our next chapter reviews RDA section 8 on recording relationships between resources.

RDA Section 8:
Resource-to-Resource Relationships

Having identified the persons, families, or corporate bodies associated with our resource, we now look at the relationship of our resource to other resources. This is the final step of our RDA to MARC workflow for bibliographic descriptions.

Step 7: Record the Relationships of the Resource to Other Resources
- RDA section 8: chapters 24–28
- MARC 5xx, 7xx, (8xx, 490)

RDA Markers

Look for these symbols as you move through the text:

☐　　Identifies RDA core, LC core, and PCC core elements ☐

✪　　Starred LC-PCC policy statements ✪

Δ　　Notes changes in rules and practice from AACR2 Δ

✚　　Marks new MARC fields or changes in practice ✚

☉　　Targets/Locates cataloging practices within RDA's text ☉

SECTION 8

Recording Relationships between Works, Expressions, Manifestations, & Items

Section 8: Recording Relationships between Works, Expressions, Manifestations, and Items	
Chapter	Title
24	General Guidelines on Recording Relationships *between Works, Expressions, Manifestations, and Items*
25	Related Works
26	Related Expressions
27	Related Manifestations
28	Related Items

Section 8 addresses the relationships between works, expressions, manifestations, and items. The relationships are between resource entities of the same level.

- Chapter 25: A Work to Other Works
- Chapter 26: An Expression to Other Expressions
- Chapter 27: A Manifestation to Other Manifestations
- Chapter 28: An Item to Other Items

Chapter 24: General Guidelines

24.3 Core Elements

There are no RDA core relationships in section 8. Some relationships are identified as LC or LC/PCC core in policy statements in chapters 25–28. We'll look at each of them as we go.

24.4 Recording Relationships between Works, Expressions, Manifestations, and Items

The relationships can be expressed in the following ways:

- As an identifier for the related entity (not used alone)
- As an authorized access point (only for a work or expression)
- As a structured description
- As an unstructured description

Structured descriptions occur in formatted fields, such as linking entry fields (MARC 76x–78x) and in formatted contents notes in MARC 505. An unstructured description provides bibliographic details in free text, without specific formatting. They are often found in general notes (e.g., MARC 500). See RDA 24.4.3.

24.4.1 Identifier for the Related Work, Expression, Manifestation, Item

◒ LC-PCC PS: Do not use an identifier alone.

24.5 Relationship Designator

RDA instructs catalogers to use relationship designators given in Appendix J for the relationships covered in chapters 25–28 and recorded in bibliographic records (e.g., in 7xx fields, $i). The use of relationship designators from Appendix J is encouraged in the PCC guidelines (PCC 2013, [3]). However, if the element is considered sufficient (for expressing the relationship), designators are not necessary (Appendix J.1). In some cases, the MARC coding of the bibliographic record represents the relationship, and some libraries do not add designators. Further, unstructured descriptions may contain text or terms that explain the relationship (24.5.1.3) and thus would not require separate designators. Finally, do not use Appendix J terms in authority records.

⊙ This is the only place in section 8 where use of Appendix J is mentioned. The appendix is not specified in the separate chapters on works (25), expressions (26), manifestations (27), or items (28).

Appendix J is divided into sections that correspond to the separate chapters in section 8:

J. 2—Related Works
J. 3—Related Expressions
J. 4—Related Manifestations
J. 5—Related Items

Chapter 25: Work-to-Work Relationships

Chapter 25 covers relationships between the work being described and other works. Related works may be cited in a bibliographic record and may also be related within an authority record as a see also reference.

◒ LC-PCC PS 25.0, Purpose and Scope: There is a lengthy LC-PCC policy statement at 25.0, with two main parts:

- Guidelines on work-to-work relationships between musical and literary or art works
- PCC guidelines for authorized access points and numbering for series

25.1. Related Work

Work-to-work relationships include adaptations, compilations, commentaries, supplements, sequels, and whole-part relationships (25.1.1.1 Scope). The policy statement at 25.1 differentiates LC practice from PCC practice, as outlined below.

LC-PCC PS 25.1: LC Practice

⨂ ☐ Work-to-work relationships are LC core for three situations:

Compilations (whole-to-part relationship)
- To express the whole-to-part relationship for compilations, provide a 505 contents note, listing all titles unless burdensome.
- Provide an analytical authorized access point (MARC 7xx) for the predominant or first work (if substantial).
    - Use the relationship designator "container of (work)" (MARC 7xx subfield 'i'). See Appendix J.2.4, Whole-Part Work Relationships.

See chapter 21 of the book for additional information on compilations.

Serial Relationships (e.g., continues/continued by)
- For the serial relationship "continuation of/continued by" use structured descriptions in MARC 780 (continuation of) and 785 (continued by) fields (Appendix J.2.6, Sequential Work Relationships).
- Include identifiers in the structured description, as available:
    - subfield 'x' = ISSN of related title
    - subfield 'w' = LCCN of related title (qualified as DLC)
    - subfield 'w' = OCLC record number (qualified as OCoLC)

Commentaries That Include the Work Commented On (6.27.1.6 and LC-PCC PS 25.1)
If a commentary (that contains the original work) is described using the commentary title as the title proper, then a relationship to the original work should be included. The relationship designator "commentary on" is found in Appendix J.2.3, Descriptive Work Relationships.

⨂ *LC-PCC PS 25.1: PCC Practice*

PCC follows LC practice for compilations, with two additions.
- ◉ PCC practice covers adding regular tables of contents notes at 25.1.
- For compilations, PCC optionally gives analytical authorized access points for additional parts/titles.

⨂ 25.1.1.3 LC-PCC PS provides LC/PCC guidelines for formatting formal content notes.

Chapter 26: Expression-to-Expression Relationships

26.1 Related Expression:

A related expression is described as an expression related to the expression being described. Revised versions of a work, translations, abridgements, or new editions have an expression-level relationship to the original.

✪ ☐ LC-PCC PS 26.1: Related expressions are LC/PCC Core for:

- Compilations
- Serial relationships

Examples
- A compilation comprised of translated titles
- Serials in different language editions
- Serials with sequential relationships such as "continuation of/continued by"

Expression level relationships for compilations and serials are handled similarly to those for works. To record the expression-level aspect of a translation/language edition relationship, add $1 <language> to the analytical entry created for the related work.

Chapter 27: Related Manifestations (Reproductions)

Related manifestations are other manifestations that are related to the manifestation being described. They can include various reproductions (facsimiles, reprints), manifestations of the work issued in other formats, and other manifestations issued with the described manifestation (such as "filmed with" or "issued with" materials). The examples in RDA show these relationships represented with a structured or unstructured description, or with an identifier.

✪ ☐ *LC-PCC PS 27.1:*

Related manifestation is an LC/PCC core element for reproductions. The policy statement defines reproductions as including republications, reprints, reissues, and facsimiles.

> "The word "reproduction" is being used in its broadest sense to include all resources formerly identified as reproductions, republications, reprints, reissues, facsimiles, etc., that still represent equivalent content between an original resource and a reproduction of that original. Revised editions represent different expressions and are not treated as reproductions."

27.1.1.3 Recording Relationships to Related Manifestations

✪ LC-PCC PS: LC/PCC Practice*: When a separate bibliographic record is created for a reproduction, express its relationship to the original manifestation using:

- MARC 775, Other edition linking entry
  - If the reproduction is in the same format, or,
- MARC 776, Additional physical form entry
  - if the reproduction is in a different format, or,

- MARC 500 for bibliographic history note
  - If no structured description of the original is available

MARC 775/776 contain a structured description of the original manifestation + subfield 'i' "Reproduction of (manifestation)" from Appendix J.4.2, Equivalent Manifestation Relationships.

If there is no existing record on which to base the 775/776 description of the original manifestation, use a 500 bibliographic history note.

Do not use this approach if you are using a "single record" or "provider-neutral" records.

✪ PCC has noted problems with RDA's treatment of reproductions. The LC-PCC Policy statement at 27.1.1.3 states that they are forming a task group to look into the issue.

Chapter 28: Related Items (Bound With and Reproductions)

28.1 Related Item

Item-to-item relationships exist when a specific, single instance of a resource (an item) is the basis for the relationship to a second item. Resources with item-to-item relationships will often be local to a specific agency. RDA gives the example of an item used as the basis for a microform reproduction.

✪ ☐ LC-PCC PS 28.1: Related item is core for LC for reproductions:

- "When it is important to identify the specific item" used for reproduction
- For "bound with" materials

28.1.1.3 Recording Relationships to Related Items

✪ The LC-PCC PS at 28.1.1.3 discusses how to create references for related items.

- Use the MARC 775 (same format) or 776 (different format) when it is important to cite the relationship of a reproduction to its original item. Use the relationship designator "reproduction of (item)" from Appendix J.5.2.
- Locally "bound with" materials should be related using a structured description in a 501 note. Designate the relationship "With" in subfield 'a'.

CONCLUSION

This chapter concludes our RDA into MARC workflow. In the next chapter, we look at RDA sections 3 and 9, which deal more directly with authority work than bibliographic description. Section 3 covers attributes of persons, families, and corporate bodies, and section 9 talks about the relationships between them.

15

RDA Sections 3 and 9: Authority Work

Chapter 14 completed the RDA into MARC workflow for the bibliographic description. Chapter 15 looks at two RDA sections that are used mainly for authority work but might be used when constructing access points to enter in bibliographic descriptions.

- RDA section 3, chapters 8–11: attributes of person, family, corporate body
- RDA section 9, chapters 29–32: relationships between persons, families, and corporate bodies

RDA Markers

Look for these symbols as you move through the text:

☐　　Identifies RDA core, LC core, and PCC core elements ☐

✪　　Starred LC-PCC policy statements ✪

Δ　　Notes changes in rules and practice from AACR2 Δ

✚　　Marks new MARC fields or changes in practice ✚

⊙　　Targets/Locates cataloging practices within RDA's text ⊙

SECTION 3

Recording Attributes of Person, Family, & Corporate Body

Section 3: Recording Attributes of Person, Family, and Corporate Body	
Chapter	Title
8	General Guidelines on Recording Attributes of Persons, Families, and Corporate Bodies
9	Identifying Persons
10	Identifying Families
11	Identifying Corporate Bodies

Section 3 deals predominantly with recording attributes of persons, families, or corporate bodies and constructing authorized access points for them. In our MARC environment this is mostly recorded as authority data. Remember, though, that section 6 (Recording Relationships to Persons, Families, and Corporate Bodies) references section 3 (see chapter 13 of the book). Section 6 tells us what relationships to record and then points us to section 3 for guidelines on how to construct the access points with which to express the relationships.

Chapter 8

As the first chapter in the section, chapter 8 provides general information and guidelines on recording attributes of these group 2 FRBR entities.

Chapters 9, 10, 11

Chapter 9 offers guidelines for identifying persons, chapter 10 for identifying families, and chapter 11 for identifying corporate bodies. The three chapters are similarly organized.

The approach used in these chapters may feel a bit reminiscent of that used for chapter 6, where we identified a preferred title in order to name a work and construct an authorized access point for it. Here we will identify the preferred name for a person, family, or corporate body and use it to construct an access point to represent them.

Example: Chapter 9, Identifying Persons

For example, chapter 9 provides guidelines for preferred name at 9.2.2, and then guidelines for access points at 9.19.1.

- 9.2.2 Preferred Name for the Person
- 9.19.1 Authorized Access Point Representing a Person

9.2–9.18

Between 9.2 and 9.18, the attributes that can be used to identify a person are listed. Some of these attributes can be used to qualify the authorized access point for a person in order to differentiate it from all others. (See 9.19.1.3.–9.19.1.7.) When added to the bibliographic record in an access point, professions and other designations are enclosed in parentheses. (Schiff "Changes . . . Part 2," 19)

> 9.19.1.3 Date of Birth and/or Death
> 9.19.1.4 Fuller Form of Name
> 9.19.1.5 Period of Activity of the Person and/or Profession or Occupation
> 9.19.1.6 Other Term of Rank, Honor, or Office
> 9.19.1.7 Other Designation

Any of these, or the other attributes, may be added to authority records, often in specific MARC fields. Their inclusion as authority data is frequently left to the cataloger's judgment.

9.19

When you get to 9.19, the guidelines for constructing access points refer back to the instructions for the individual attributes. For example, at 9.19.1.3, Date of Birth and/or Death, you are referred back to date of birth (9.3.2), and/or date of death (9.3.3).

A look at the table of contents shows that chapters 10 and 11 are organized similarly, with attributes for each entity described at the beginning of the chapters and guidelines on constructing access points using the attributes following.

SECTION 9

Recording Relationships between Persons, Families, & Corporate Bodies

Section 9: Recording Relationships between Persons, Families, and Corporate Bodies	
Chapter	Title
29	General Guidelines on Recording Relationships *Between Persons, Families, Corporate Bodies*
30	Related Persons
31	Related Families
32	Related Corporate Bodies

Section 9 presents guidelines on recording *relationships between* persons, families, and corporate bodies. The relationships can be between persons, between a person and a family, or other combinations as shown below.

- Person to person
- Person to family
- Person to corporate body
- Family to family
- Family to corporate body
- Corporate body to corporate body

The relationships described in section 9 will be recorded primarily as MARC authority data in the form of references.

Chapter 29

Chapter 29 offers general guidelines on recording relationships between persons, families, and corporate bodies. There are no core relationships defined by RDA. There are some LC or PCC core elements as designated in LC-PCC policy statements in chapters 30–32. An identifier and/or an authorized access point may be used to express these relationships. (❂ See 29.4.1 LC-PCC PS—don't use an identifier on its own.)

29.4 Recording Relationships Between Persons, Families, and Corporate Bodies

Both rule 29.4.1, Identifier for the Related Person, Family, or Corporate Body, and rule 29.4.2, Authorized Access Point Representing the Related Person, Family, or Corporate Body, send catalogers to section 3 (chapters 9, 10, and 11) for guidelines on recording identifiers and constructing authorized access points for persons, families, and corporate bodies.

29.5 Relationship Designator

Use of relationship designators for these relationships is optional and left to the cataloger's judgment. If used, they are listed in Appendix K. They are entered in authority records in 5xx (see also from) references. The relationship designator is recorded in subfield 'i'. Be sure to include subfield 'w' = r (Library of Congress, "RDA: Module 4," 18).

Chapters 30, 31, 32

Chapters 30, 31, and 32 offer guidelines for recording relationships of persons, families, or corporate bodies associated with a related person (chapter 30), a related family (chapter 31), or a related corporate body (chapter 32).

These relationships are not core in RDA and are optionally recorded. However, there are two relationships designated as LC/PCC core.

- ○□ LC-PCC PS 30.1: Related persons are core for "different identities." These would be pseudonymous relationships (a person who uses different names).
- ○□ LC-PCC PS 32.1: Sequential relationships for immediately preceding/ succeeding corporate bodies are core elements for LC/PCC at RDA 32.1.

CONCLUSION

This concludes our review of RDA's ten main sections and how they are used in developing a MARC-encoded bibliographic record.

The next section of the book (chapters 16 through 23) is designed as ready reference help for using RDA. It features charts on RDA's contents and RDA changes to MARC, and chapters on special topics such as collaborations or use of the MARC 33x fields. The book concludes with a selection of MARC examples for a variety of formats.

Part Three

Special Topics and Examples

16

RDA Quick Reference Table of Contents

PART ONE: RECORDING ATTRIBUTES

Section 3: Recording Attributes of Person, Family, and Corporate Body	
Chapter	Title
8	General Guidelines on Recording Attributes of Persons, Families, and Corporate Bodies
9	Identifying Persons
10	Identifying Families
11	Identifying Corporate Bodies

◻ *Chapters 8–11 are used to construct access points for persons, families, and corporate bodies. They deal mostly with authority data. Resulting access points may be added to bibliographic records.*

Section 4: Recording Attributes of Concept, Object, Event, and Place		
Chapter	Title	Note
12	General Guidelines	
13	Identifying Concepts	*To be developed after the initial release of RDA*
14	Identifying Objects	
15	Identifying Events	
16	Identifying Places	

PART TWO: RECORDING RELATIONSHIPS

Section 5: Recording Primary Relationships between Work, Expression, Manifestation, and Item	
Chapter	Title
17	General Guidelines on Recording Primary Relationships
LC-PCC PS—Do not apply in current implementation scenario	

Section 9: Recording Relationships between Persons, Families, and Corporate Bodies	
Chapter	**Title**
29	General Guidelines on Recording Relationships *between Persons, Families, Corporate Bodies*
30	Related Persons
31	Related Families
32	Related Corporate Bodies

□ *Chapters 29–32 describe relationships between persons, families and corporate bodies. The relationships are recorded as references (e.g., variant forms) in authority records.*

Section 10: Recording Relationships between Concepts, Objects, Events, and Places	
Chapter	**Title**
33	General Guidelines on Recording Relationships *between Concepts Objects, Events, and Places*
34	Related Concepts
35	Related Objects
36	Related Events
37	Related Places

To be developed after the initial release of RDA

APPENDICES, GLOSSARY, INDEX

RDA's "Back Matter"	
Appendices	
A	Capitalization
B	Abbreviations and Symbols
C	Initial Articles
D	Record Syntaxes for Descriptive Data
E	Record Syntaxes for Access Point Control
F	Additional Instructions on Names of Persons
G	Titles of Nobility, Terms of Rank, Etc.
H	Dates in the Christian Calendar
Appendices—Relationship Designators	
I	Relationships **between** a Resource (Work, Expression, Manifestation, Item) **and** Persons, Families, and Corporate Bodies Associated with the Resource
J	Relationships **between** Works, Expressions, Manifestations, Items: Work to Work, Expression to Expression, Manifestation to Manifestation, and Item to Item
K	Relationships **between** Persons, Families, and Corporate Bodies
L	Relationships **between** Concepts, Objects, Events, and Places
Glossary	
	A–Z
Index	
	A–Z
RDA Update History	
2012 April Update	
	2012 Update Summary
	Instruction Archive
2013 July Update . . . etc.	

17

RDA into MARC Overview:
Quick Reference Chart

RDA INTO MARC: A NEW WORKFLOW

Using RDA, the process for creating a bibliographic description follows the general workflow outlined below. This workflow was discussed in chapter 9. It is reproduced here as a quick reference tool.

RDA into MARC: A New Workflow

RDA INTO MARC WORKFLOW

Record Attributes of Manifestation and Item

Step 1. Identify the Manifestation and Item
  • RDA section 1: chapter 2
  • MARC 245, 246, 3xx, 4xx, 5xx

Step 2. Describe Carrier Elements
  • RDA section 1: chapter 3
  • MARC 337, 338, and 300a, 300c

Step 3. Provide Acquisitions and Access Information
  • RDA section 1: chapter 4
  • MARC 02x, 856

Record Attributes of Work and Expression

Step 4. Identify the Work and Expression/Assign Content Type
  • RDA section 2: chapter 6
  • MARC 100/110/111, 130, 240, (245), 7xx, 8xx
  • MARC 336 (Content Type)

Step 5. Describe Content
  • RDA section 2: chapter 7
  • MARC 300a, 300b, 5xx

Identify Relationships

Step 6: Record the Relationships of the Resource to Persons, Families, or Corporate Bodies
  • RDA section 6: chapters 18–22
  • MARC 100, 110, 111, 700, 710, 711

Step 7: Record the Relationships of the Resource to Other Resources
  • RDA section 8: chapters 24–28
  • MARC 5xx, 7xx, (8xx, 490)

Authority Sections

- Section 3: Recording Attributes of Persons, Families, and Corporate Bodies
  - Chapters 8–11 deal with the attributes used to create access points for persons, families, and corporate bodies.
  - Much of the data is recorded in authority records.
  - The access points created using the guidelines may be entered in bibliographic records.

- Section 9: Recording Relationships between Persons, Families, and Corporate Bodies
  - These chapters (29–32) provided guidelines on expressing relations between persons, families, and corporate bodies, which are mostly recorded within the authority reference structure.

Not Applied

- Section 5: Recording Primary Relationships between Work, Expressions, Manifestations, and Items
  - This section (chapter 17) is not being applied in LC's initial implementation of RDA.

Not Written

- Section 4: Recording Attributes of Concepts, Objects, Events, and Places
  - Chapters 12, 13, 14, 15 are not yet written, and will deal with creating access points for subjects (concepts, objects, events).
  - Chapter 16, Places, does exist and deals with creating access points for places.

- Section 7: Recording Relationships to Concepts, Objects, Events, and Places
  - Chapter 23 is not yet written. It will cover the relationships between a work and its subjects.

- Section 10: Recording Relationships between Concepts, Objects, Events, and Places
  - Chapters 33–37 have not been written. They will cover relationships between subject entities and likely be recorded as authority references.

MARC Chart: RDA Impacts

The following chart notes MARC bibliographic fields impacted by RDA. It does not list every MARC field, but only those noteworthy for RDA. Fields are included when

- They are newly created for RDA.
- Subfields have been added for RDA.
- Mapping from RDA elements to MARC is of note.
- RDA practice impacts use of the MARC field.

Where the chart references "LC R5" it is referring to the Library of Congress training document "MARC 21 encoding to accommodate RDA elements: LC practice." It is available on the Library of Congress RDA Training Materials website. MLA recommendations cited in the chart refer to the Music Library Association's "Best Practices for Music Cataloging: Using RDA and MARC 21" (version 1.0, February 21, 2014).

MARC Bibliographic Fields and RDA Practice

MARC	MARC Field Name and RDA Practice	RDA Rule/Comments
LDR		
/06	**Type of record** Codes available at: www.loc.gov/standards/value list/rdacontent.html	6.9 Content type (code) New as RDA element See also MARC 336
/07	**Bibliographic level** 'm' for single unit and multipart monograph 's' serial and 'I' integrating resource	2.13 Mode of Issuance (code) New as RDA element
/18	**Description** = i (ISBD) if ISBD punctuation is used	Should not be 'a' AACR2
007	Physical description fixed field	
/00	**Category of material** Codes available at: www.loc.gov/standards/valuelist/rdamedia.html	3.2 Media type (code) New as RDA element See also MARC 337
/01	**Specific material designation** Codes available at: www.loc.gov/standards/valuelist/rdacarrier.html New codes added: • Code k—computer card *in* Electronic Resources • Code d—disc, type unspecified *in* Electronic Resources • Code e—disc cartridge, type unspecified *in* Electronic Resources • Code h—microfilm slip *in* Microform • Code j—microfilm roll *in* Microform • Code f—other or unspecified type of filmstrip *in* Projected graphic • Code a—activity card *in* Nonprojected graphic • Code k—poster *in* Nonprojected graphic • Code p—postcard *in* Nonprojected graphic • Code q—icon *in* Nonprojected graphic • Code r—radiograph *in* Nonprojected graphic • Code s—study print *in* Nonprojected graphic • Code v—photograph, type unspecified *in* Nonprojected graphic • Code o—film roll *in* Motion picture	3.3 Carrier type (code) New as RDA element See also MARC 338

/04	New codes for Nonprojected Graphic; Physical Medium for Map, Globe: • Code v—leather • Code w—parchment • Code n—vellum • Code i—plastic • Code l—vinyl	RDA 3.6 Base Material (for these new codes)
008	Fixed-length data elements	
/06	**Type of date/Publication status** When 264$c copyright date is provided, code /06 as 't'—publication date and copyright date	RDA 2.7-2.11 Publication, etc., and Copyright date
/07–10	**Date 1** When 264$c copyright date is provided, Publication (or etc.) date entered here	RDA 2.7-2.11 Publication, etc., and Copyright date
/11–14	**Date 2** When 264$c copyright date is provided, Copyright date entered here	RDA 2.7-2.11 Publication, etc., and Copyright date
/20	**Format of music** New codes added for Music, 008/20: • Code h—chorus score • Code i—condensed score • Code j—performer-conductor part	
028	**Publisher Number** $q (qualifier) , e.g., (disc 1).	
033	**Date/Time and Place of an Event** New subfields: $p—Place of event $0—Record control number—LC does not use, see LC's R5–MARC 21 changes document $2—Source of term given in $p	RDA 7.11 Place and date of capture See also MARC 518 LC—prefer 518 (see R5)
040 $b	**Language of cataloging:** $b Specify the language of cataloging here, including 'eng' for English	
040 $e	**Description conventions:** $e rda (preferred subfield order = a, b, e, c, d)	

046	**Special Coded Dates:** $o Single or starting date for aggregated content $p Ending date for aggregated content	RDA 6.4 and 6.10 LC: use in authority records; not in bib- liographic records (R5)
100$e/4 110$e/4 111$j/4 700$e/4 710$e/4 711$j/4	**Main Entry Fields 1xx, Added Entry Fields 7xx** Creators, Others: Name to resource relationship $e Relationship designator, x00, x10 $j Relation- ship designator, x11 $4 Relationship code Use Appendix I.2. Do not use in 7xx name/title headings.	RDA 18.5, 19.2, 19.3 PCC Guidelines, 04/2013 –Use relationship desig- nators for all Creators. –Don't use $4 code if $e term (or x11$j) is provided.
245 $a	Title Statement Transcribe what you see, including errors. Set library policy re: capitalization	RDA 2.3
245 $h Do Not Use	**Title Statement $h [Medium] or GMD** RDA replaces the General Material Designation with Content, Media, and Carrier data. See MARC 336, 337, 338	RDA 6.9, 3.2, 3.3
250	**Edition Statement** Transcribe what you see on resource, no abbreviations	RDA 2.5.1.4
260 ·	**Publication, Distribution, etc. (Imprint)** *"Information in field 260 is similar to information in field 264 (Production, Publication, Distribution, Manufacture, and Copyright Notice). Field 260 is useful for cases where the content standard or in- stitutional policies used do not make a distinction between functions." MARC 21 Bib Formats 260*	See new 264 fields
264 #0	Production statement—NEW for RDA $a Place, $b Name, $c Date	RDA 2.7

264 #1	**Publication statement—NEW for RDA** $a Place, $b Name, $c Date	RDA 2.8
264 #2	**Distribution statement—NEW for RDA** $a Place, $b Name, $c Date	RDA 2.9
264 #3	**Manufacture statement—NEW for RDA** $a Place, $b Name, $c Date	RDA 2.10
264 #4	**Copyright notice date—NEW for RDA** $c Date	RDA 2.11
300	**Physical Description—RDA implications:** $a Extent—RDA manifestation attribute $b Other physical details—some RDA expression attributes for content are recorded here $c Dimensions—RDA manifestation attribute *May have multiple 300 fields.*	RDA 3.4—Extent 7.2—Duration RDA 7.15, 7.17—Color/Illustrative Content RDA 3.5—Dimensions
336	**Content Type—NEW for RDA** $a Term $b Code $2 Source ($2 rdacontent) *MARC allows for multiple terms from same vocabulary to be entered in one field in repeated subfields. Many agencies prefer to use separate 336 fields to record multiple terms.*	RDA 6. 9—Expression-level attribute RDA provides list of terms Also coded in LDR/06
337	**Media Type—NEW for RDA** $a Term $b Code $2 Source ($2 rdamedia) *MARC allows for multiple terms from same vocabulary to be entered in one field in repeated subfields. Many agencies prefer to use separate 337 fields to record multiple terms.*	RDA 3.2—Manifestation attribute RDA provides list of terms Also coded in 007/00
338	**Carrier Type—NEW for RDA** $a Term $b Code $2 Source ($2 rdacarrier) *MARC allows for multiple terms from same vocabulary to be entered in one field in repeated subfields. Many agencies prefer to use separate 338 fields to record multiple terms.*	RDA 3.3—Manifestation attribute RDA provides list of terms Also coded in 007/01

340	Physical Medium—NEW subfields for RDA: $j—Generation [NEW, 2011] $k—Layout [NEW, 2011] $m—Book format [NEW, 2011] $n—Font size [NEW, 2011] $o—Polarity [NEW, 2011] $0—Authority record control number or standard number [NEW, 2011] $2—Source [NEW, 2011]	
344	Sound Characteristics—NEW for RDA Carrier	RDA 3.16
345	Projection Characteristics of Moving Image—NEW for RDA Carrier	RDA 3.17
346	Video Characteristics—NEW for RDA Carrier	RDA 3.18
347	Digital File Characteristics—NEW for RDA Carrier	RDA 3.19
377	Associated Language—NEW for RDA $a Language code $l Language term $2 Source	RDA 6.11 Language of Expression In bibliographic records, use to identify the language in which a work is expressed, or language used by creator
380	Form of Work	RDA 6.3 LC uses in authority record (R5)
381	Other Distinguishing Characteristics of a Work or Expression	RDA 6.12 LC uses in authority record (R5)

382	**Medium of performance**	RDA 6.15 LC prefers data in authority, may also enter in bibliographic record.
383	**Numeric designation of musical work**	RDA 6.16 LC uses in authority record (R5)
384	**Key**	RDA 6.17 LC uses in authority record (R5)
490	**Series Statement**—$x is repeatable Allows for recording ISSNs for both series and subseries	RDA 2.12
501	**Bound with note**—Item to item relationship	RDA 28.1.1.3
502	**Dissertation note**—new format for notes $b Academic degree $c Granting institution/faculty $d Year degree granted	RDA 7.9.2, 7.9.3, 7.9.4
505	**Contents note:** Work to work relationship	RDA 25.1.1.3 LC-PCC PS
518	**Date/Time and Place of an Event Note field:** $d—Date of event [NEW, 2010] $o—Other event information [NEW, 2010] $p—Place of event [NEW, 2010] $0—Record control number [NEW, 2010] $2—Source of term [NEW, 2010]	RDA 7.11 Place and Date of Capture Field 033 contains same information in coded form. Note may be parsed into new fields, or be given in $a as free text.

588	**Source of Description Note** NEW field added in 2009	RDA 2.17.13 Note on Issue, Part, or Iteration Used as the Basis for Identification of the Resource
700$e/4 710$e/4 711$j/4	**Added Entry—Name** Contributors: Name to resource relationship $e Relationship designator (700, 710) $j Relationship designator (711) $4 Relationship code (700, 710, 711) Use Appendix I Do not use in name/title headings	RDA 20.2 PCC Guidelines, 04/2013 –"Highly encourages" using designators for all access points. –Don't use $4 code if $e (or x11$j) is provided.
700 710 711 740	**Added Entry—Name/Title (700, 710, 711)** **Added Entry—Uncontrolled Title (740)** Resource to resource relationship (work, expression) for: Analytic entries for contents of compilations Other relationships (e.g., parody, abridgement, etc.) Translations (expression level) Use Appendix J when a relationship designator is added in $i	RDA chapter 25 (Related works) RDA chapter 26 (Related expressions) Appendix J
765	**Original Language Entry** Resource to resource relationship (expression)— Structured description Could be used to record relationship of resource (translation) to its original language expression	RDA chapter 26 (Related expressions)

775 776	**Other Edition Entry (775)** **Additional Physical Form Entry (776)** Resource to resource relationship (manifestation)—Structured Relationship between a reproduction and its original 775 when reproduction is same format as original 776 when reproduction is a different format Use Appendix J.4.2, Equivalent Manifestation Relationships for $i relationship designator	RDA chapter 27 (Related manifestations) Appendix J.4.2
780/785	**Preceding (780)/Succeeding (785) Entry** Resource to resource relationship (work, expression)—Structured Serial relationships "continues, continued by" Use Appendix J.2.6 or J.3.6 (Sequential Work/Expression Relationships) if adding designator to $i	RDA chapter 25 (Related works) RDA chapter 26 (Related expressions) Appendix J
787	**Other Relationship** (formerly Nonspecific Relationship)—redefined Often used with a 580 note.	RDA Section 8—Resource to Resource relationships

MARC 264 Fields and Publication Dates

RDA RULES 2.7–2.11: EXPANDED
PUBLICATION, ETC. ELEMENTS

Where AACR2 combined publication, distribution, and manufacture information into a single "Publication, Distribution, Etc. Area," RDA parses them into separate elements and rules. It also designates separate elements for production data (for unpublished materials) and copyright date.

MARC 264 AND RDA 2.7–2.11

A new, repeatable field, 264, was created in MARC to accommodate the new RDA elements. Field 264 supplements field 260 and is called the Production, Publication, Distribution, Manufacture, and Copyright Notice field. The second indicator code identifies what is being recorded in a given 264 field. (See MARC 264 2d Indicator Values)

MARC 264 2d Indicator Values

MARC 264 Production, Publication, Distribution, Manufacture, and Copyright Notice Field	
MARC 264 1st__ 2d Indicators	2d indicator = Function of entity (RDA data elements recorded)
#__0	Production
# __1	Publication
#__ 2	Distribution
# __3	Manufacture
#__ 4	Copyright notice date

Note: In our discussion, we will use the pound sign (#) value as the first indicator. Other values for the first indicator are possible. See LC MARC 21 Bibliographic Formats.

Within the MARC field 264, subfield 'a' designates place, subfield 'b' provides the name, and subfield 'c' is used to record dates. The copyright notice date uses only subfield 'c' for date.

MARC 264 Subfields

MARC 264 Subfield	Data Recorded	Notes
a	Place	of production, publication, distribution, manufacture
b	Name	of producer, publisher, distributor, manufacturer
c	Date	of production, publication, distribution, manufacture, or copyright notice

Examples

A resource identified as being published by Little, Brown, in Boston, Massachusetts, in 2010 would have a 264 field that looked like the following. The second indicator '1' designates publication data.

264   # 1 $a Boston : $b Little, Brown, $c 2010.

A resource containing a copyright date of 2013 could have a 264 field as follows:

264   # 4 $c ©2013

LC GUIDELINES ON RDA 2.7–2.11

The Library of Congress has developed guidelines on how to prioritize and record data pertaining to these elements. In a nutshell, they encourage catalogers to supply publication place and date whenever feasible. The guidelines are given in LC-PCC Policy Statements at the appropriate rules (most notably at 2.8.2.6 and 2.8.6.6). They are also covered in the training manual for Module 1 (Library of Congress, "RDA: Module 1," 19–31).

LC Guidelines on Place of Publication (RDA 2.8.2)

The first-named place of publication is an RDA core element.

LC follows RDA as to source of information and transcription for places of publication. For sources, take the place of publication from the same source as the publisher's name, another source in the resource, or another outside source as specified at instruction 2.2.4.

Place(s) of publication should be transcribed as they appear (2.8.1.4), including the local name and the larger jurisdiction. There is an optional addition to add a larger jurisdiction if it is lacking and judged as needed for clarification (2.8.2.3).

RDA allows for recording all places of publication listed on the source of information.

Neither LC nor RDA follows the AACR2 provision to choose as place of publication the place that is located in the agency's "home" country (2.8.2.4).

If a place of publication is not identified on the resource, RDA and LC encourage supplying a place from another source (2.8.2.6). An LC-PCC Policy Statement at 2.8.2.6 advises catalogers to supply a "probable" place of publication rather than use RDA's [place of publication not identified] phrase. Supplying the probable country of publication is preferred over no place identified (see 2.8.2.6.3, known country, and 2.8.2.6.4, probable country).

> **Note:** For supplied data, RDA differentiates between "known" and "probable." Known means that you found a source that stated the information, even though it's not the preferred source of information. This data should be given in brackets or given a note as to source (2.2.4). Probable means the data is uncertain and should be both bracketed and question-marked, for example, [San Francisco?].

LC Guidelines on Publisher Name (RDA 2.8.4)

Publisher name is an RDA core element. Only the first name is required in RDA.

Sources of information for publisher name, in order, are the same source as for the title proper, elsewhere in the resource, or other sources as defined at 2.2.4.

Publisher names should be transcribed as they appear (2.8.1.4). RDA provides an optional omission to leave out corporate levels (hierarchy), but an LC-PCC Policy Statement at 2.8.4.3 recommends including them.

If you choose to record multiple publisher names when more than one publisher is given on the resource, rule 2.8.4.5 says to record them in the order indicated by sequence, and so on.

Unlike place of publication, if no publisher name can be identified from the resource or other sources, catalogers are not encouraged to supply one. Record [publisher not identified] in these cases (RDA 2.8.4.7).

LC Guidelines on Date of Publication (RDA 2.8.6)

Date of publication is an RDA core element.

LC's guidelines on supplying dates of publication go into great depth on what to do when there is no date of publication for a single-part resource (LC-PCC PS 2.8.6.6).

Per RDA 2.8.6.2, date of publication information can be taken from (in order) the same source as the title proper, another source within the resource, or an outside source as specified at 2.2.4.

Dates of publication are recorded as they appear, per 2.8.6.3 and 2.8.1, with reference to the rule at 1.8, "General guidelines on numbers expressed as numerals or as words." Rule 1.8.2, Form of Numerals, instructs us to record numerals in the form preferred by the agency. There are two alternatives: first, to record numerals as they appear, and second, to record numerals as they appear and add the equivalent numerals preferred by the agency. In an LC-PCC Policy Statement, LC catalogers are instructed to apply the first alternative. Hence, LC catalogers transcribe a date of publication in Roman numerals if that is how they appear.

At 2.8.6.6, RDA instructs catalogers to supply a date or approximate date of publication when none can be found on a single-part resource. Information on formatting supplied dates is offered at 1.9.2. (See RDA Supplied Date Formats, MARC 264)

RDA Supplied Date Formats, MARC 264

RDA	Type of Supplied Date	Format
1.9.2.1	Actual date known	[2002]
1.9.2.2	One of two consecutive years	[1997 or 1998]
1.9.2.3	Probable year	[1892?]
1.9.2.4	Probable range of years	[between 1984 and1986?]
1.9.2.5	Earliest/Latest possible date	[not before May 2014]

In the LC-PCC Policy Statement at 2.8.6.6, LC describes five scenarios for supplied dates of publication.

A. Use a copyright date as the supplied date of publication (in brackets, in the 264 #1 $c) if there is only a copyright date and either
   a. Copyright date is likely the publication date,
      Or,
   b. Copyright date is for the following year in which the publication was received.
   c. Optionally record the copyright date as a copyright date element in 264 #4 $c.
B. Use the copyright date as the supplied date of publication (in brackets, in 264 #1 $c):
   a. If the copyright date and manufacture date are the same.
C. Use the copyright date as the supplied date of publication (in brackets, in 264 #1 $c):
   a. If the copyright date is different from the manufacture date.
   b. Optionally record the manufacture date in 264 #3 $c, or as a note on issue, part, or iteration (MARC 588, RDA 2.17.13).
D. If there is only a distribution date:
   a. Use it as the supplied date of publication (in 264 #1 $c, in brackets) if it is a likely publication date.
   b. Do not use it if it does not seem reasonable. Supply a date of publication (such as a range of dates) based on the information you have (record in 264 #1 $c, in brackets).
   c. Optionally record the distribution date as a distribution date element in 264 #2 $c.
E. If there is only a manufacture date:
   a. Use it as the supplied date of publication (in 264 #1 $c, in brackets), if it is reasonable that the manufacture date is the publication date. Optionally record the manufacture date as part of the manufacture statement (264 #3 $c).
   b. Do not use it if it does not seem likely to be the publication date. Supply a date of publication (264 #1 $c, in brackets) based on the information you have. Optionally record the manufacture date in the manufacture statement (264 #3 $c) or as a note (MARC 588, RDA 2.17.13).

20

Content, Media, and Carrier Types in MARC 33x

RDA does away with the General Material Designator (GMD). In AACR2, the GMD was recorded in square brackets in the title field (245 subfield 'h'). It was often useful but also presented problems. Sometimes it was not specific enough and it sometimes described content and at other times, carrier information. To address the issue, RDA's developers worked with the publishing community to replace the GMD with three new elements—content type, media type, and carrier type. These elements are related to data that publishers use in ONIX metadata (JSC 2006 [1]).

Content Type (RDA core)—MARC 336

- Definition:
  Content type is the fundamental form of communication in which content is expressed and the human sense through which it is perceived. For images, it includes spatial dimensions. It is an expression-level attribute.
- Where in RDA?
  RDA 6.9—Guidelines for recording content type are found here. A closed vocabulary list of terms, with definitions, is included here.
- LC Term and Code List for RDA Content Types:
  LC provides a freely available online chart of content terms and codes to be entered in MARC 336 subfields $a (terms) and $b (codes). The chart also includes the corresponding LDR/06 codes for content.

Media Type (LC/PCC Core)—MARC 337

- Definition:
  Media type is the general type of intermediation device required to view, play, run, etc., the content of a resource.
- Where in RDA?
  RDA 3.2—Guidelines for recording the media type are found here. A closed vocabulary list of terms, with definitions, is included.
- LC Term and Code List for RDA Media Types:
  LC provides a chart of content terms and codes to be entered in MARC 337 subfields $a (terms) and $b (codes). The chart also includes the corresponding 007/00 codes.

Carrier Type (RDA core)—MARC 338

- Definition:
  Carrier type is the format of the storage medium and housing of a carrier in combination with the type of intermediation device.
- Where in RDA?
  RDA 3.3—Guidelines for recording carrier type are found here. A closed vocabulary list of terms, with definitions, is also found here.
- Term and Code List for RDA Carrier Types:
  LC provides a chart of carrier terms and codes to be entered in MARC 338 subfields $a (terms) and $b (codes), as well as corresponding codes for 007/01.

The lists of terms at 6.9, 3.2, and 3.3, are closed lists. If no term is appropriate, catalogers are instructed to record "other." If type can't be determined or is unknown, catalogers should record "unspecified."

MARC coding for all three fields is similar:

$a term $b code $2 source $3 materials specified

When RDA's lists of terms are used, subfield 2 is recorded as follows:

336 $2 rdacontent
337 $2 rdamedia
338 $2 rdacarrier

RDA 3.2.1.3, 3.3.1.3, and 6.9.1.3 instruct catalogers to record multiple terms for content, media, and carrier, if applicable. There are alternatives at each rule to record a single term reflecting the predominant part, or multiple terms describing the most substantial parts, of the resource.

When using multiple terms, best practice leans toward using multiple fields (e.g., multiple 336 fields) rather than stringing terms in one field with multiple subfields. MARC formats allow for either.

Subfield '3' (materials specified) can be used to specify what part of the resource is described by the terms in the field. It can be useful when you have multiple pieces in a resource and are including multiple fields and terms. For example:

336 _ _ $3 Blu-ray $a two-dimensional moving image $2 rdacontent
336 _ _ $3 booklet $a text $2 rdacontent

The following chart presents common triplets of content, media, and carrier terms and codes for various formats. (See MARC 33x Fields)

MARC 33x Fields

Resource	336 $a Content Term	336 $b Code	337 $a Media Term	337 $b Code	338 $a Carrier Term	338 $b Code
Book	text	txt	unmediated	n	volume	nc
Picture Book	text, still image	txt, sti	unmediated	n	volume	nc
Graphic Novel	text, still image	txt, sti	unmediated	n	volume	nc
Print Thesis	text	txt	unmediated	n	volume	nc
ETD (E-thesis)	text	txt	computer	c	online resource	cr
DVD	two-dimensional moving image	tdi	video	v	video disc	vd
Blu-ray	two-dimensional moving image	tdi	video	v	video disc	vd
Music CD	performed music	prm	audio	s	audio disc	sd
Spoken Word CD	spoken word	spw	audio	s	audio disc	sd
Download Audiobook	spoken word	spw	computer	c	online resource	cr
E-book	text	txt	computer	c	online resource	cr
Video Game (disc)	two-dimensional moving image	tdi	computer	c	computer disc	cd
Online Integrating Resource	text *Could have other content terms	txt	computer	c	online resource	cr
E-Journal	text	txt	computer	c	online resource	cr
Streaming Video	two-dimensional moving image	tdi	video (optional), computer	v, c	online resource	cr
Streaming Audio	Music: performed music (and/or) Word: spoken word	prm, spw	audio (optional), computer	a, c	online resource	cr

21

Collaborations and Compilations

COLLABORATIVE WORKS

RDA addresses collaborative works at 6.27.1.3. Treat a work as a collaboration when two or more persons, families, or corporate bodies are together responsible for creating it. Collaborators can be creators whether they perform the same or different roles in a work, as specified at RDA 19.2.1.1.

6.27.1.3

Construct the authorized access point representing a collaborative work by combining (in this order):

a) The authorized access point representing the person (see 9.19.1), family (10.10.1), or corporate body (11.13.1) with principal responsibility
b) The preferred title for the work (6.2.2)

If there are multiple creators with equal responsibility, record the first named (in 1xx).

Exception: For works created by one or more corporate bodies (see 19.2.1.1.1) along with one or more persons or families, select the principal corporate body as creator plus the preferred title to form the authorized access point for the work.

Additional exceptions are given for these specific formats: moving image works, musical collaborations, and treaties.

Notes on Collaborations

Δ In AACR2, if no principal creator was identified, entry would be under title. In RDA, the first or principal creator is entered in 1xx, and others may be entered as 7xx added entries.

Δ Access points for any number of additionally named creators can be recorded (no more Rule of Three). In MARC, they are given in 7xx fields.

✪ LC-PCC Policy Statement at 19.3: No other 7xx authorized access points are required, but any number may be added per the cataloger's judgment.

COMPILATIONS OF WORKS

RDA addresses compilations of works by one entity and compilations by multiple entities in separate sections of chapter 6.

Compilations by One Entity
- 6.2.2.10: Recording the Preferred Title for a Compilation of Works of One Person, Family, or Corporate Body
- 6.27.1.2: [Constructing Access Points for] Works Created by One Person, Family, or Corporate Body

Compilations by Multiple Entities
- 6.27.1.4: Compilations of Works by Different Persons, Families, or Corporate Bodies

Compilations also appear in chapter 25, as whole/part work-to-work relationships.

- 25.1 LC-PCC Policy Statement—Related work is a core element for LC for compilations.

Also note this statement at 19.2.1.1 Basic Instructions on Recording Creators, Scope:

> In some cases, the selection, arrangement, editing, etc., of content for a compilation effectively results in the creation of a new work. When this occurs, the person, family, or corporate body responsible for compiling the aggregate work may be considered to be the creator of the compilation.

COMPILATION OF WORKS OF ONE PERSON, FAMILY, OR CORPORATE BODY

6.2.2.10 Recording the Preferred Title for a Compilation of Works of One Person, Family, or Corporate Body
- If the work is "known by" a title, use that title (6.2.2.4).

If not:

6.2.2.10.1 Complete Works

- Use the conventional collective title "Works" for complete works (MARC 240).
- For the authorized access point, include the creator.

6.2.2.10.2 Complete Works in a Single Form

- Use a specific conventional collective title (e.g., Poetry, Novels, Essays) in MARC 240.
- Include the creator in the authorized access point for the work.

6.2.2.10.3 Other Compilations of Two or More Works, But Not All Works, by One Creator

RDA instructs the cataloger to record the preferred title for each of the works, but LC follows the alternative at 6.2.2.10.3 to use a conventional collective title, followed by Selections.

- Use the format <Conventional collective title>. $k Selections (MARC 240).
- Provide a 700 name/title access point for the first or predominant work or expression (see LC-PCC Policy Statement 25.1/26.1).
- 700s for additional titles are optional (cataloger's judgment).

25.1 Related Works: LC-PCC Policy Statement

Related work is a core element for LC for compilations:

- Give a MARC 505 contents note unless the contents are indicated in another part of the description.
- There is no limit on the number of titles in the contents note unless burdensome.

Notes on Compilations

Δ If a compilation is a selection of plays by one author, use "Plays $k Selections" as the preferred title. Unlike in AACR2, you don't need to determine if the creator produced works in one or multiple formats (e.g., did she write just plays, or poetry and plays?).

Δ "Selections" is not used as a collective title, but is always subordinate in subfield 'k'.

Δ If there is no "known by" title, always use a conventional collective title for the preferred title. Unlike in AACR2, you don't need to consider whether title proper is a distinctive title.

Δ No longer add a date for compilations whose preferred title is a collective title beginning with "Works."

COMPILATIONS BY DIFFERENT PERSONS, FAMILIES, OR CORPORATE BODIES

6.27.1.4 Compilations of Works by Different Persons, Families, or Corporate Bodies

Use the preferred title of the work to construct the authorized access point. Do not add a creator. The preferred title will be:

- Title by which the compilation is known, or
- Title proper (manifestation-level title)

19.1.2 Recording Persons, Families, and Corporate Bodies Associated with a Work:

If the resource is an aggregate containing two or more works, and each is asso-ciated with different persons, families, or corporate bodies, record the persons, families, and corporate bodies associated with each of the works.

19.2 Only the Principal or First-named Creator Is Required

LC-PCC Policy Statement—Use cataloger's judgment on whether to re-cord additional creators.

Optionally provide analytical authorized access points for the separate works in a compilation (700 name/title).

25.1 Related Works: LC-PCC Policy Statement

Related work is a core element for LC for compilations:

- Give a MARC 505 contents note unless the contents are indicated in another part of the description.
- There is no limit on the number of titles in the contents note unless burdensome.

Compilations Lacking a Collective Title

If the compilation lacks a collective title, RDA says to construct separate access points for the works in the compilation (6.27.1.4). An RDA alterna-tive gives the option to use a devised title in these cases. LC and PCC do not generally apply the alternative (LC-PCC PS 6.27.1.4). As explained in their training materials, LC applies its policy statement at 25.1, Related Work, in this situation (Library of Congress, "RDA: Module 2," 22).

- Use the title proper of the first work as the preferred title of the work, re-corded in the title proper (245 $a).
- Provide an analytical authorized access point for the predominant or first work (700 name/title).

- Optionally provide analytical authorized access points for the other titles (700 name/title).

Notes

Δ For works lacking a collective title, RDA uses title entry, with analytical entries for at least the first and optionally for additional titles. AACR2 would identify the work with a MARC 240 field (uniform title) for the first work, and record the author of the first work as the principal creator in the 1xx field. An analytical entry for the additional title(s) would be made.

As well as being in RDA's instructions and policy statements, LC covers these topics in its training materials (Library of Congress, "RDA: Module 2," 21–22).

Note Fields in RDA

We have seen that everything in RDA is structured around FRBR entities (works, expressions, manifestations, and items). This approach holds true for notes as well. Instructions on adding notes are distributed throughout RDA in the appropriate section pertaining to the relevant FRBR entity. Notes that deal with attributes of manifestations or items are covered in section 1. Notes that pertain to works or expressions appear in section 2.

Notes may also express relationships. Guidelines for one such situation are found in section 8, Recording Relationships between Works, Expressions, Manifestations, and Items. At chapter 24.4, Recording Relationships, rule 24.4.3 tells us that we can use an "unstructured description" to record relationships. An unstructured description is essentially a note, as the glossary and examples at 24.4.3 suggest. (A structured description is also sometimes given as a note.)

Unlike AACR2, access points in RDA may be included in a bibliographic description without an explanation appearing elsewhere in the record. Hence, notes that would be required to justify an entry in AACR2 are optional in RDA. By and large, notes are not core elements in RDA, although LC-PCC Policy Statements specify several notes as core or core if.

WHERE ARE INSTRUCTIONS ON NOTES IN RDA?

The RDA bibliographic mappings, RDA to MARC, and its opposite, MARC to RDA, show which elements have been mapped to 5xx notes fields. (The mappings are freely available from the Tools tab at http://access .rdatoolkit.org.) Clusters of notes occur in the following chapters:

- Chapter 2.17: Note on Manifestation
- Chapter 2.21: Note on Item
- Chapter 3: Describing Carriers
- Chapter 7: Describing Content
- Chapter 25.1: Related Work (MARC 505 Contents Note)

Chapter 2.17, Note on Manifestation

You will find a group of notes in chapter 2.17 that are familiar from AACR2. They deal with characteristics of a manifestation. When other rules in chapter 2 direct catalogers to make notes, they generally point to section 2.17 for details. For example, at 2.8.1.5.2, Changes in Publication Statement for Serials, RDA instructs catalogers to "Make a note (see 2.17.7.5.2) if. . . ."

Chapter 3, Describing Carriers

The elements in chapter 3, Describing Carriers, are divided between being mapped to the MARC 300 physical description field, one of the MARC 34x fields, and/or to a MARC 5xx note field. For some, the data may additionally be encoded in the MARC 007 field. The MARC 340 field, Physical Medium, was enhanced for RDA to record some of these characteristics and a group of additional 34x fields were also created. Best practices are still developing. In some cases, data previously recorded in MARC 5xx notes may now be recorded in one of the MARC 34x fields, but some will remain in notes fields.

Chapter 7, Describing Content

Many of the attributes that describe the content of works or expressions in chapter 7 are mapped to various 5xx notes fields in MARC. Here again, the elements listed will strike a familiar chord with AACR2 cataloging. Some elements, such as illustrative and color content, are primarily recorded in MARC 300$b, but may also merit general notes in a MARC 500 note field.

Chapter 25.1, Related Work

There is one significant note here—the contents note—that is described in the LC-PCC Policy Statement at 25.1. The contents note expresses the whole-part relationship of chapters or titles (for a compilation)—the parts—to the work as a whole.

According to LC-PCC Policy Statement 25.1, a contents note in MARC 505 is LC core for compilations, with no limit on titles unless burdensome. PCC practice is to "give complete contents in a MARC 505 contents note unless considered burdensome or unless the contents are indicated in another part of the description."

RDA Examples

The following examples come from a variety of sources and libraries, including the Library of Congress. Many have been shortened to highlight those fields impacted by RDA. Coded and fixed fields have largely been excluded, and identifying information, such as the 040 cataloging agency code, has been removed. The records represent real-time cataloging examples of RDA. They may not include every field that could be included in an RDA record, but should generally include core elements for their specific formats.

SINGLE VOLUME MONOGRAPH—ONE AUTHOR— EXAMPLE #1

```
LDR     01177cam a2200313 i 450
040 _ _  $a XXX $b eng $c XXX $e rda
100 1 _  $a Quindlen, Anna.
245 1 0  $a Still life with bread crumbs : $b a novel / $c Anna Quindlen.
250 _ _  First edition.
264 _ 1  $a New York : $b Random House, $c [2014]
300 _ _  $a 252 pages ; $c 25 cm
336 _ _  $a text $2 rdacontent
337 _ _  $a unmediated $2 rdacontent
338 _ _  $a volume $2 rdacarrier
```

RDA Notes

Leader position 18 = 'i' for ISBD punctuation. Should not be 'a' for AACR2.

040     $b eng: Specify language of cataloging, including English.
040     $e rda: Specify that you are following RDA for cataloging.

Preferred order is $a, $b, $e, $c, $d

100   Creator: No relationship designator in this record. Some libraries (and some earlier RDA records) do not use relationship designators for authors in the 100

field. PCC policy advocates using relationship designators for all creators (PCC 2013, [1]).

250   Edition: "First edition" is spelled out as it appears on the source of information (RDA 2.5.1.4 Recording Edition Statements, 2.5.2.3 Recording Designation of Edition, Appendix B Abbreviations, B.4 Transcribed Elements).

264 _ 1 Publication Statement (RDA 2.8.1, MARC 21 Format for Bibliographic Data)
- MARC coding, second indicator '1' identifies this information as publication information.
- $c [2014]: Bracketed date signifies that the publication date was supplied. It may be that a copyright date appeared on the source and was used as the supplied date of publication (LC practice).

300   Physical Description/Extent
- RDA 3.4.5, subfield 'a' "pages" is spelled out.
- RDA 3.5.1.4.14, subfield 'c' ".cm" is recorded as a symbol, with no ending punctuation.

336   Content Type, RDA 6.9, RDA core
337   Media Type, RDA 3.2, LC core
338   Carrier Type, RDA 3.3, RDA core

The 33x fields replace the GMD (formerly in 245 $h).
The three terms "unmediated volume of text" describe a book.

SINGLE VOLUME MONOGRAPH—ONE AUTHOR—EXAMPLE #2

```
020 _ _  $a 9781742610764 (paperback) : $c $19.99
040      $a AAA $b eng $ e rda $d AAA
100 1_   $a Tiffany, Carrie, $e author.
245 10   $a Mateship with birds / $c Carrie Tiffany.
264 _1   $a Sydney : $b Picador, $c 2012.
264 _4   $c ©2012
300 _ _  $a 211 pages ; $c 21 cm
336 _ _  $a text $2 rdacontent
337 _ _  $a unmediated $2 rdacontent
338 _ _  $a volume $2 rdacarrier
586 _ _  $a The Stella Prize 2013 Winner ; NSW Premier's Literary Awards 2013 Winner.
```

RDA Notes

020    $c $19.99: Recording price is addressed in RDA chapter 4: Providing Acquisition and Access Information. See rule 4.2.1.3.

100   Creator "$e author": This library has used the relationship designator "author" from Appendix I.2.1. It is recorded in subfield 'e'.

264 _4 Copyright Date: When the copyright date is the same as the date of publication, some libraries do not record it, while others have opted to do so. This record includes the copyright date. RDA uses the copyright symbol, © (RDA 2.11.1.3).

586   Award Note: RDA chapter 7, Describing Content, RDA 7.28 Award

CHILDREN'S PICTURE BOOK—EXAMPLE #1

```
100 1_   $a French, Jackie, $e author.
245 10   $a Baby wombat's week / $c written by Jackie French ; illustrated by Bruce Whatley.
264 _1   $a Sydney : $b Angus & Robertson, $c 2013.
```

264 _4 $c ©2009
300 _ _ $a 30 unnumbered pages : $b color illustrations ; $C 21 X 29 cm
336 _ _ $a text $2 rdacontent
336 _ _ $a still image $2 rdacontent
337 _ _ $a unmediated $2 rdamedia
338 _ _ $a volume $2 rdacarrier
500 _ _ $a First published in Australia in 2009
520 _ _ $a The star of the bestseller Diary of a Wombat is back – with a new mouth
          to feed. Cuter, stroppier, and even more determined than her mother . . . meet
          Mothball's baby. Age 3 +.
521 _ _ $a For children.
586 _ _ $a Australian Book Industry Awards Winner.
700 1 _ $a Whatley, Bruce, $e illustrator.

RDA Notes

300     $a, RDA 3.4.5.3 option 'a' is used here, "unnumbered pages." LC prefers option
        (c). Policy statement at 3.4.5.3.
300     $b Other Physical Details, "color illustrations": Illustrative content is recorded
        here per RDA 7.15 Illustrative content. Color content is recorded per RDA
        7.17.1.3. As the RDA to MARC Bibliographic Mapping states at 7.17.1,
        "MARC combines a range of characteristics, using free text" in the MARC 300
        subfield 'b.'
336     $a still image

Some libraries include a second content type term (336 $a still image) to represent the illustrations in picture books, as is done here (RDA 6.9).

520   Summary: Summarization of the content is a core element for LC for fiction
        intended for children. LC-PCC Policy Statement 7.10.
521   Audience: Intended audience is a core element for LC for resources intended for
        children. LC-PCC Policy Statement 7.7.
700   Added Entry—Personal Name: Illustrators are considered to be contributors in
        RDA. The LC-PCC Policy Statement at 20.2.1.3 states that the first illustrator is
        LC core for resources for children.

CHILDREN'S PICTURE BOOK—EXAMPLE #2

100 1 _ $a Eppard, Jon.
245 1 0 $a Dogs / $c written by Jon Eppard ; illustrated by Steve Porter.
264 _1 $a Minneapolis, MN : $b Bellwether Media, $c 2013.
300 _ _ $a 24 pages : $b illustrations ; $c 24 cm.
336 _ _ $a text $2 rdacontent
337 _ _ $a unmediated $2 rdamedia
338 _ _ $a volume $2 rdacarrier
490 0 _ $a You can draw it!
504 _ _ $a Includes bibliographical references (page 23) and index.
520 _ _ $a "Information accompanies step-by-step instructions on how to draw dogs.
          The text level and subject matter is intended for students in grades 3 through
          7"—Provided by publisher.
700 1 _ $a Porter, Steve, $e illustrator.

RDA Notes

100   Creator: Note there is no relationship designator in the 100 field. PCC best
        practice is to add a designator for creators (PCC 2013, [1]).
300     $c "24 cm.": Note that "cm." ends with punctuation. This is a full stop required
        by ISBD punctuation because of the 490 series field that follows (Library of
        Congress, "RDA: Module 2," 6).
336   Content type: In this example, only one content type (for text) is provided (RDA
        6.9).
504   Bibliography: Bibliographies and indexes are considered supplementary content
        in RDA (7.16.1.1). The LC- PCC Policy Statement at 7.16.1.3 instructs catalog-
        ers to use a 504 note for bibliographies.
520   Summary: The summary includes the intended audience, more often seen in
        MARC 521. LC-PCC Policy Statement at 7.7 and 7.10.

COLLABORATION

100 1_ $a Hampson, Tim, $e author.
245 10 $a World beer / $c Tim Hampson with Stan Hieronymus, Sylvia Kopp, and
           Adrian Tierney-Jones ; foreword by Sam Calagione, Dogfish Head Brewery.
250 _ _ $a First American edition.
264 _ 1 $a London : $b DK, $c 2013.
300 _ _ $a 300 pages : $b color illustrations ; $c 29 cm
336 _ _ $a text $2 rdacontent
337 _ _ $a unmediated $2 rdamedia
338 _ _ $a volume $2 rdacarrier
500 _ _ $a Includes index.
700 1_ $a Hieronymus, Stan, $e author.
700 1_ $a Kopp, Sylvia, $e author.
700 1_ $a Tierney-Jones, Adrian, $e author.

RDA Notes

100     $a: Collaborative works 6.27.1.3. Authorized access point for the work is the
        preferred title *with the authorized access point for the [person] with principal
        responsibility.*
245     $c Statement of Responsibility: Four people with primary responsibility are
        recorded. RDA allows for recording as many entities as are listed. It provides an
        option to follow AACR2's Rule of Three, if desired. See RDA 2.4.1.5.
245     $c Foreword by Sam Calagione. Dogfish Head Brewery: If there is more than
        one statement of responsibility, record them in order indicated (RDA 2.4.1.6).
700     $a, $e: This library has chosen to optionally record additional creators and
        to include relationship designators from I.2.1 (Recording Creators 19.2.1.3,
        Example "Two or More Persons, Families, or Corporate Bodies Responsible for
        the Creation of the Work Performing the Same Role," LC-PCC Policy Statement
        19.2 Creator, RDA to MARC mapping 19.2).

The library chose not to include an access point for Sam Calagione, who wrote the foreword.

COMPILATION—TWO NOVELS BY THE SAME AUTHOR

100 1 _ $a Hilderbrand, Elin.
240 10 $a Novels. $k Selections

245 10 $a One summer : $b two novels / $c Elin Hilderbrand.
250 _ _ $a 1ˢᵗ ed.
264 _1 $a New York : $b St. Martin's Griffin, $c 2013.
300 _ _ $a ix, 618 pages ; $c 21 cm
336 _ _ $a text $2 rdacontent
337 _ _ $a unmediated $2 rdamedia
338 _ _ $a volume $2 rdacarrier
505 0 _ $a The Blue Bistro – The love season.
700 1 2 $a Hilderbrand, Elin. $t Blue Bistro.
700 1 2 $a Hilderbrand, Elin. $t Love season.
740 0 2 $a Blue Bistro.
740 0 2 $a Love season.

RDA Notes

100/240   Authorized Access Point for the Work: For compilations of some, but not all, works by one author, this record follows the alternative at 6.2.2.10.3 and the LC-PCC Policy Statement at 6.2.2.10.3. Use a conventional collective title, "Novels," followed by subfield 'k' "Selections." The creator is recorded as part of the authorized access point (RDA 6.27).

505   Content note: The LC-PCC Policy Statement at 25.1 instructs catalogers to give a 505 contents note for compilations.

700 1 2   Name/Title entry: LC practice requires a name/title entry for the predominant or first-named title when it represents a substantial part of the resource for compilations of works (LC-PCC Policy Statement 25.1).
  • The second name/title entry in this record is optional. It makes sense from a user's point of view to add both in this record. PCC practice is to add these access points "if considered important for access" (LC-PCC Policy Statement 25.1, PCC practice).

740   Added Entry/Uncontrolled Related/Analytical Title: Following the alternative at 6.2.2.10.3, these entries are optional in RDA.

COMPILATION—COMPLETE WORKS

100 0 _ $a Sappho, $e author.
240 1 0 $a Works. $l English
245 1 0 $a Sappho : $b a new translation of the complete works / $c Diane Rayor, Andre Lardinois.

RDA Notes

100/240   Authorized Access Point for the Work/Expression: For compilations of all works by one author, LC uses the conventional collective title "Works" and includes the creator to construct the authorized access point (RDA 6.2.2.10.1).

240   $l English: In this record, the work in question is translated from Ancient Greek. The 240 is the preferred title for the work and, by adding subfield 'l' language, for the expression (6.27.3 and LC-PCC PS 6.27.3).

COMPILATION BY DIFFERENT PERSONS, FAMILIES, CORPORATE BODIES

245 00 $a Our Boston : $b writers celebrate the city they love / $c edited by Andrew Blauner.

264 _1 $a Boston : $b Houghton Mifflin Harcourt, $c 2013.

300 _ _ $a xii, 353 pages ; $c 22 cm

336 _ _ $a text $2 rdacontent

337 _ _ $a unmediated $2 rdamedia

338 _ _ $a volume $2 rdacarrier

505 0_ $a Foreword: Running toward the bombs / Kevin Cullen — Walking an American avenue / Mike Barnicle — A boy's Boston / Charles McGrath — Things in threes / Madeleine Blais — Getting over Boston / George Howe Colt — Accents, or the missing r/ Susan Orlean — Bonfire of the memories / David M. Shribman — A city not on a hill / Joan Wickersham — Our chowder / David Michaelis.

700 1 _ $a Blauner, Andrew.

RDA Notes

No 1xx, only 245 field:

For compilations of works by different persons, RDA 6.27.1.4 tells us to "construct the authorized access point representing the work by using the preferred title for the compilation." No creator is used in the authorized access point.

505   Contents: Required in LC per policy statement at 25.1
(Note: Contents have been shortened for this display)

700   Added Entry/Name: The first named or principal person associated with a work is required (in this case Andrew Blauner as editor). Additional entries are left to cataloger judgment. RDA 19.2.

LARGE PRINT BOOK—EXAMPLE #1

020 _ _ $a 9781611738865 (large print : library binding : alk. paper)

100 10 $a Paine, Lauran.

245 10 $a Prairie Empire : $bA Western Story /$c Lauran Paine.

250 _ _ $a First Edition.

264 _1 $a Thorndike, Maine : $b Center Point Large Print, $c 2013.

300 _ _ $a 190 pages (large print) ; $c 23 cm

336 _ _ $a text $2 rdacontent

337 _ _ $a unmediated $2 rdamedia

338 _ _ $a volume $2 rdacarrier

650 _0 $a Large type books.

LARGE PRINT BOOK—EXAMPLE #2

020 _ _ $a 9781611736861 (library binding : acid-free paper)

040 _ _ $a JKL $b eng $c JKL $e rda $d JKL

100 1 0 $a Nye, Nelson C. $q (Nelson Coral), $d 1907–1997.

245 1 4 $a The bandit of Bloody Run /$c Nelson Nye.

250 _ _ $a Large print edition.

264 _ 1 $a Thorndike, Maine : $b Center Point Large Print, $c 2013.

264_ 4 $c ©1939

300 _ _ $a 238 pages (large print) ; $c 23 cm

[33x fields deleted from example, see example 1)
650 _ 0 $a Large type books.

RDA Notes

RDA doesn't change much with large print books, except for those libraries who used a GMD for them. The 33x fields do not address large type.

LC continues to use (large print) in the 300 $a field.

The RDA to MARC mapping offers three options for recording font size. See RDA, Describing Carriers, Recording Font Size, at RDA 3.13.1.3 and the MARC mappings.

- 300 $a   Extent: e.g., $a 23 pages (large print).
- 340 $n   Large print, or 340 $n large print (point size): e.g., $n large print (18 point).
- 500 $a   General note: e.g., $a Large print book.

Few libraries are using the 340 $n at this time. Most prefer the LC practice of including (large print) in the 300$a.

GRAPHIC NOVEL

100 1 _ $a Colfer, Eoin, $e author.
245 10 $a Artemis Fowl. $p The eternity code : $b the graphic novel / $c adapted by Eoin Colfer & Andrew Donkin ; art by Giovanni Rigano ; color by Paolo Lamanna ; color separation by Studio Blinq ; lettering by Chris Dickey.
246 3 0 $a Eternity code
250 _ _ $a First edition.
264 _ 1 $a New York : $b Disney/Hyperion Books, $c 2013.
300 _ _ $a 1 volume, unpaged : $b chiefly color illustrations ; $c 23 cm
336 _ _ $a text $b txt $2 rdacontent
336 _ _ $a still image $b sti $2 rdacontent
337 _ _ $a unmediated $b n $2 rdamedia
338 _ _ $a volume $b nc $2 rdacarrier
520 _ _ $a After Artemis uses stolen fairy technology to create a powerful microcomputer and it is snatched by a dangerous American businessman, Artemis, Juliet, Mulch, and the fairies join forces to try to retrieve it.
700 1 _ $aDonkin, Andrew, $e author.
700 1 _ $a Rigano, Giovanni, $e illustrator.
700 1 _ $a Lamanna, Paolo, $d 1973- $e colorist.
700 1_ $a Dickey, Chris, $e illustrator.

RDA Notes

100    $a Creator: The first-named or principal creator of the graphic novel is generally recorded in the 100 field. Recommended to apply the appropriate relationship designator in $e, e.g., $e author.

300    $a Extent: If a graphic novel does not have numbered pages record "1 volume, unpaged" for its extent. See RDA 3.4.5.3, option 'c'.

300    $b Other physical details: Specify illustrations here as well as color content. LC often uses "chiefly illustrations" or "chiefly color illustrations" to describe the illustrated nature of graphic novels. The 300 subfield 'b' combines two elements of Describing Content (chapter 7): Illustrative content (7.15) and Color content (7.17).

336   Content Type (RDA 6.9): Most graphic novels are described using two content types:
- 336 $a   text
- 336 $a   still image

520   Summary: Graphic novels that are children's fiction should include a summary (LC-PCC Policy Statement at 7.10).

700   Added Entry/Personal Names
- The principal illustrator should be recorded in a 700 field, with the relationship designator "illustrator." See LC-PCC Policy Statement at 20.2.1.3.
- Additional names may optionally be recorded.

THESIS—ARCHIVAL HARD COPY

LDR   00000ntm 2200000Ki 4500
100 1 _ $a Smith, Victor M., $e author.
245 10 $a Isolation of soy-bean farmers / $c by Victor M. Smith.
264 _ 0 $a [Columbus] : $b Ohio College of Farming, $c 2013.
300 _ _ $a iii, 45 pages : $b illustrations ; $c 28 cm
336 _ _ $a text $2 rdacontent
337 _ _ $a unmediated $2 rdamedia
338 _ _ $a volume $2 rdacarrier
502 _ _ $b B. S. $ c Ohio College of Farming, $d 2013.
504 _ _ $a Includes bibliographical references.
700 2_ $a Lobel, William R. $q (William Robert), $e thesis advisor.

ELECTRONIC THESIS

LDR   00000nam 2200000Ki 4500
100 1 _ $a Riddler, Corrine, $e author.
245 1 0 $a Climatology and creationism : $b implications for North American pine forests / $c by Corrine Riddler.
264 _ 1 $a [Boston] : $b Nashville College, $c 2013.
300 _ _ $a 1 online resource (iii, 333 pages) : $b PDF, illustrations, map.
336 _ _ $a text $2 rdacontent
337 _ _ $a computer $2 rdamedia
338 _ _ $a online resource $2 rdacarrier
500 _ _ $a Title from first page of PDF file.
502 _ _ $b B.S. (Honors) $c Nashville College $d 2012.
504 _ _ $a Includes bibliographical references (pages 28–33)
530 _ _ $a Available online via college's Online Thesis Viewer.
538 _ _ $a System requirements: World Wide Web and PDF viewer
700 1 _ $a Collins, Jerome, $e thesis advisor.

RDA Notes

264 _0   Production Statement for Unpublished Resources

Best practice appears to agree that the archival copy of a thesis or dissertation is an unpublished resource.

Date is RDA core and should be recorded. Place and Name of producer are not core.

264 _1   Publication Statement for Published Resources

Electronic and print reproductions of theses/dissertations are considered to be published. Place, name, and date are RDA core. Bracket supplied information. Bracket and question mark probable dates.

336 Content type (RDA 6.9), 337 Media type (RDA 3.2), 338 Carrier type (RDA 3.3)

Print:
    336 text
    337 unmediated
    338 volume

Electronic:
    336 text
    337 computer
    338 online resource

502   Dissertation Note (Electronic (ETD) or Print)
- RDA includes three specific elements relating to dissertations—Academic Degree, Granting Institution or Faculty, and Year Degree Granted.
- MARC 21 accommodates the new elements in new subfields of the 502 note field—$b Degree type, $c Name of granting institution, $d Year degree granted.
- Dissertation or thesis information is considered core for LC and PCC (LC-PCC Policy Statement at 7.9).
- The LC-PCC Policy Statement at 7.9.1.3 specifies that catalogers should use the new subfields rather than the older AACR2 format. Do not use AACR2 punctuation.

776   Additional Physical Form (Linking) Entry

Although not shown in the examples here, when a print copy is made from an electronic or micro-format, it is a reproduction in a different format. In these cases, include a 776 field, with the relationship designator "$i Reproduction of (manifestation)" (RDA 27.1 and LC-PCC PS 27.1.1.3).

REPRODUCTION (SAME FORMAT)—775 STRUCTURED DESCRIPTION

041 1 _ $a rus $h eng
100 1 _ $a Carroll, Lewis, $d 1828–1898, $e author.
240 10 $a Alice's adventures in Wonderland. $l Russian
245 10 $a Soniả v tšarstvie diva = |b Sonja in a kingdom of wonder : a facsimile of the first Russian translation of "Alice's adventures in Wonderland" / |c by Lewis Carroll ; introduction by Nina Demurova ; edited by Mark Burstein.
264 _ 1 $a Mhaigh Eo, Éire : |b Evertype ; |a [New York] : |b Lewis Caroll Society of North America, |c 2013.
300 _ _ $a ix, xv, iv, 177 pages : |b illustrations, facsimiles ; |c 22 cm
336 _ _ $a text $2 rdacontent
337 _ _ $a unmediated $2 rdamedia
338 _ _ $a volume $2 rdacarrier
700 1 _ $a Demurova, N. M. |q (Nina Mikhaĭlovna), |d 1930- |e writer of supplementary textual content.
700 1 _ $a Burstein, Mark, |d 1950- |e editor.
775 08 $i Facsimile of (manifestation): |a Carroll, Lewis, 1832–1898. |s Alice's adventures in Wonderland. Russian. |t Soniả v tsarstvie diva. |d Moskva : Tip. A.I. Mamontova, 1879 |w (OCoLC)79682743

REPRODUCTION (SAME FORMAT)—500 BIBLIOGRAPHIC HISTORY NOTE

100 1 _ $a Northrop, Eugene P. $q (Eugene Purdy), $d 1908–1969, $e author.
245 10 $a Riddles in mathematics : $b a book of paradoxes / $c Eughen P. Northrop ; introduction by Daniel S. Silver.
250 _ _ $a Dover edition.
264 _ 1 $a Mineola, New York : $b Dover Publications Inc., $c 2014.
300 _ _ $a 288 pages ; $c 21 cm
336 _ _ $a text $2 rdacontent
337 _ _ $a unmediated $2 rdamedia
338 _ _ $a volume $2 rdacarrier
500_ _ $a Reprint of: Princeton, New Jersey : D. Van Nostrand Company, Inc., 1944.

RDA Notes

First Example

775   Other Edition (Linking) Entry: A reproduction of a particular manifestation of a work is considered related to the original manifestation. When a separate record approach is used, the relationship is LC/PCC core. It is expressed in a 775, 776, or 500 MARC field. See LC-PCC Policy Statements at 27.1 and 27.1.1.3 policy statement.

When there is a structured description for the original manifestation available:

• MARC 775 is used when the format is the same (e.g., print to print).
• MARC 776 is used when the format is different (e.g., print to microform).

Include identifiers for the structured description (OCLC#, LCCN, etc.) in subfield 'w'.
Relationship designators for subfield 'i' in MARC 775/776 are selected from Appendix J.4.2 Equivalent Manifestation Relationships.

Second Example

When there is no structured description available, record information about the original manifestation (bibliographic history) in a 500 note (RDA 27.1.1.3).

TRANSLATIONS AND LANGUAGE EDITIONS

041 1_ $a eng $h fre
100 1 _ $a Moundlic, Charlotte.
240 10 $a Slip de Bain, ou, Les pires vacances de ma vie. $l English
245 14 $a The bathing costume, or, The worst vacation of my life /$c by Charlotte Moundlic ; illustrated by Olivier Tallec ; translated by Claudia Zoe Bedrick.
246 30 $a Bathing costume
246 30 $a Worst vacation of my life
250 _ _ $a First American edition.
264 _1 $a New York : $b Enchanted Lion Books, $c 2013.
300 _ _ $a pages cm
336 _ _ $a text $2 rdacontent
337 _ _ $a unmediated $2 rdamedia
338 _ _ $a volume $2 rdacarrier
500 _ _ $a Originally published: France : Flammarion, © 2011 under the title: Le Slip de Bain, ou, Les pires vacances de ma vie.

520 _ _ $a On his first vacation without his parents, eight-year-old Myron faces a scary grandfather, teasing older cousins, his first dive off the ten-foot board, and his grandmother's encouragement to write his mother daily, telling her of his adventures.

700 1_ $a Tallec, Olivier, $e illustrator.

700 1_ $a Bedrick, Claudia Zoe.

TRANSLATION—EXAMPLE #2

000   01211cam a22003498i 450
005   20140131...
008   140131s2014 ilu 001 1 eng
020 _ _ 9781564789037 (pbk. : alk. paper)
040 _ _ $a MMM $b eng $c MMM $e rda
041 1 _ $a eng $h fre
100 1_ $a Levé, Édouard.
240 10 $a Oeuvres. $l English
245 10 $a Works / $c Édouard Levé : Translated by Jan Steyn.
250 _ _ $a First Edition.
264 _1 $a Champaign : $b Dalkey Archive Press, $c 2014.
300 _ _ $a pages cm
336 _ _ $a text $2 rdacontent
337 _ _ $a unmediated $2 rdamedia
338 _ _ $a volume $2 rdacarrier
500 _ _ $a "Originally published in French as Oeuvres by P.O.L øditeur, Paris, 2002."
700 10 $a Steyn, Jan H., $e translator.

RDA Notes

100/240 $l Authorized Access Point for an Expression (translation)

- The LC-PCC Policy Statement at 6.27.3 instructs catalogers to identify expressions for music resources, sacred scriptures, translations, and language editions.
- Language expressions are constructed by adding the language in subfield 'l' to the authorized access point for a work (LC-PCC PS 6.27.3).
- Language of Expression is an RDA core element, as noted at 6.11, and should be used to identify an expression when applicable (0.63).

041 Language code: This field is coded as it was under AACR2.

500 Translation Note

- The derivative relationship of a translation to its original language expression can be recorded as an unstructured description in a 500 general note (RDA 26.1, MARC to RDA mapping at MARC 500). These relationships are not core (24.3).

700 Added Entry/Personal Name

- Translators are considered contributors in RDA, and are not core (RDA 20.2.1.1). PCC practice is to record contributors when "considered important for identification" (LC-PCC PS 20.2.1.3).
- The designator "translator" is found in Appendix I.3.1, Relationship Designators for Contributors.

DUAL LANGUAGE EDITION

041 1_ $a eng $a fre $h fre
100 1_ $a Proust, Marcel, $d 1871–1922.
245 10 $a Marcel Proust : $b the collected poems : a dual-language edition with parallel
            text /$c compiled by Claude Francis and Fernande Gontier ; edited with an
            introduction and notes by Harold Augenbraum.
264 _1 $a New York, NY : $b Penguin Books, $c 2013.
300 _ _ $axxvi, 352 pages ; v$cv22 cm
336 _ _ $a text $2 rdacontent
337 _ _ $a unmediated $2 rdamedia
338 _ _ $a volume $2 rdacarrier
700 1 _ $a Francis, Claude.
700 1_ $a Gontier, Fernande.
700 1_ $a Augenbraum, Harold, $e editor of compilation.
700 12 $a Proust, Marcel, $d 1871–1922.$t Poems.
700 12 $a Proust, Marcel, $d1871–1922. $t Poems. $l English.

RDA Notes

700 12 $a Proust, Marcel, $d 1871–1922. $t Poems.
700 12 $a Proust, Marcel, $d 1871–1922. $t Poems. $l English.
            • LC-PCC Policy Statement at 6.27.3: "When the original expression and one
              translation are in a compilation, give an analytical authorized access point
              for each expression." The first 700 represents the original French expression,
              using a conventional collective title "Poems." The second 700 field represents
              the English translation.

DVD—EXAMPLE #1*

245 00 $a Lee Daniels' the butler / $c Weinstein Company presents a Laura Ziskin pro-
            duction in association with Windy Hill Pictures, Follow Through Productions,
            Salamander Pictures and Pam Williams Productions ; produced by Pamela Oas
            Williams, Laura Ziskin, Lee Daniels, Buddy Patrick, Cassian Elwes ; written by
            Danny Strong ; directed by Lee Daniels.
257 _ _ $a United States $2 naf
264 _1 $a Beverly Hills, California : $b Anchor Bay Entertainment : $b Starz Media, $c
            [2014]
264 _ 4 $c ©2014
300 _ _ $a 1 videodisc (132 min.) : $b sound, color ; $c 4 3/4 in
336 _ _ $a two-dimensional moving image $b tdi $2 rdacontent
337 _ _ $a video $b v $2 rdamedia
338 _ _ $a videodisc $b vd $2 rdacarrier
344 _ _ $a digital $b optical $g surround $h Dolby Digital 5.1 $2 rda
346 _ _ $b NTSC $2 rda
347 _ _ $a video file $b DVD video $e region 1 $2 rda
380 _ _ $a Motion picture

---

* Record has been shortened by deleting multiple 7xx fields (e.g., for actors) and fields that
are the same in AACR2 and RDA. The contents of some fields (e.g., summary 520) have been
shortened.

538 _ _ $a DVD format; NTSC, region 1, anamorphic widescreen (1.85:1); Dolby Digital 5.1.
546 _ _ $a Closed-captioned; English, French or Spanish dialogue with optional Spanish subtitles and optional English subtitles for the deaf and hearing impaired.
511 1_ $a Oprah Winfrey, Mariah Carey, John Cusack, Cuba Gooding Jr., Jane Fonda.
508 _ _ $a Cinematographer, Andrew Dunn ; editor, Joe Klotz.
500 _ _ $a Based on the novel by Wil Haygood.
521 8_ $a MPAA rating: PG-13; for some violence and disturbing images, language, sexual material, thematic elements and smoking.
520 _ _ $a Inspired by a true story about Cecil Gaines, a devoted husband, father, and White House butler who served eight Presidential administrations during the turbulent politics and civil rights battles of twentieth century America.
500 _ _ $a Special features: Lee Daniels' The Butler: An American Story; the original freedom riders; deleted scenes; music video "You and I ain't nothin' no more" performed by Gladys Knight and Lenny Kravitz; gag reel.
700 1_ $a Daniels, Lee, $d 1959- $e film director,$e film producer.
700 1_ $a Strong, Danny, $d 1974- $e screenwriter.
700 1_ $a Gooding, Cuba, $c Jr., $d 1968- $e actor.
700 1_ $a Winfrey, Oprah, $e actor.
700 1_ $a Dunn, Andrew $q (Andrew William), $e cinematographer.
700 1_ $a Klotz, Joe, $e film editor.
700 1_ $a Leao, Rodrigo, $e composer (expression)
700 1_ $i Motion picture adaptation of (work): $a Haygood, Wil. $t Butler, a witness to history.

EXAMPLE #2—BLU-RAY AND DVD COMBO*

245 10 $a Indagine su un cittadino al di sopra di ogni sospetto / $c Columbia ; Daniele Senatore e Marina Cicogna presentano ; un film di Elio Petri ; produzione, Vera Film ; soggetto e sceneggiatura di Elio Petri e di Ugo Pirro ; reg{grave}ia di Elio Petri.
246 1_ $iTitle on container: $a Investigation of a citizen above suspicion
300 _ _ $a 3 videodiscs (115 min.) : $b sound, color ; $c4 3/4 in. +$e1 booklet (31 pages : color illustrations ; 18 cm)
336 _ _ $3 DVD $a two-dimensional moving image $b tdi $2 rdacontent
336 _ _ $3 Blu-ray $a two-dimensional moving image $b tdi $2 rdacontent
336 _ _ $3 booklet $a text $2 rdacontent
340 _ _ $3 DVD $b 4 3/4 in.
340 _ _ $3 Blu-ray $b 4 3/4 in.
347 _ _ $3 DVD $a video file $b DVD video $e region 1 $2 rda
347 _ _ $3 Blu-ray $a video file $b Blu-ray $e region A $2 rda
500 _ _ $a Original Italian language title presented as other title information on container: Indagine su un cittadino al di sopra di ogni sospetto.
500 _ _ $a Accompanying booklet lists the feature film's cast and credits, an essay by Evan Calder Williams, and excerpts from a 2001 book by screenwriter Ugo Pirro.
700 1_ $a Egidi, Carlo, $d 1918–1989, $e art director.
700 1_ $a Luveiller, Luigi, $d 1927–2013, $e director of photography.
700 1_ $a Cardarelli, Romano, $e production designer.
700 1_ $a Nicolai, Bruno, $d 1926–1991, $e conductor.

* Record has been shortened by deleting fields that repeat practices illustrated in example 1.

700 1_ $a Altman, Robert, $d1925–2006, $e interviewee (expression)
700 1_ $a Williams, Evan Calder, $e writer of added text.
710 2_ $a Columbia Pictures, $e production company.
710 2_ $a Criterion Collection (Firm), $e film distributor.

RDA Notes

Note: An OLAC (Online Audiovisual Catalogers) DVD/Blu-RAY Disc RDA Guide Task Force was preparing draft best practices at the time of this writing.

245   **$a Title Proper**
- Source of Information for videos is the title frame(s) or screen(s). Alternatively use a label permanently affixed to the resource (not its container) (RDA 2.2.2.3).

245   **$c Statement of Responsibility (Examples 1 & 2)**
- Include noun phrases (such as "presents") in the statement of responsibility (RDA 2.4.1.8).

246 1_   **$i Title on container (Example 2)**
- LC-PCC Policy Statement at 2.3.6.3, "Best Practices for Making Variant Titles for Other Titles Borne by an Item," Section G: If a title in another language appears on the resource, make a variant title for it.

300   **Physical Description**
- $a Extent: Give the number of units, e.g., 3 videodiscs, or 1 videodisc, (RDA 3.4.1.3, list of units at 3.3.1.3), as well as the running time/duration. Record duration in minutes, using the abbreviation "min." (RDA 7.22, Appendix B.5.3, B.7). Duration is core for LC (LC-PCC PS 7.22).
- $b Other Physical Characteristics:
  - Sound (RDA 7.18, Exception for moving images): Record "sound" or "silent."
  - Color (RDA 7.17.3.3): Record color, e.g., "black and white," "sepia," "color."
- $c Dimensions: LC-PCC Policy Statement at 3.5.1.4.4: Record the dimensions of a disc in inches, using its abbreviation "in." (Appendix B.7). See also the 340 $b field.

336   **Content Type (RDA 6.9)**
- For 336, 337, and 338, record the predominant [content, media, or carrier] type or record as many as are applicable. In Example 2, the library has recorded content types for DVD, Blu-ray, and an accompanying booklet.
- Example 2 uses subfield '3' to identify the specific parts being described (e.g., $3 DVD, $3 booklet).
- Content type for DVD and Blu-ray is "two-dimensional moving image."
- Subfield 'b' code for DVD and Blu-ray is "tdi". Codes are available at http://www.loc.gov/standards/valuelist/marccontent.html

337   **Media Type (RDA 3.2)**
- Example 1 uses subfield 'b' to record the MARC code for media type. http://www.loc.gov/standards/valuelist/marcmedia.html
- Media type for DVD and Blu-ray is "video." The MARC code is "v".

338   **Carrier Type (RDA 3.3)**
- Example 1 uses subfield 'b' to supply the MARC code for carrier type. http://www.loc.gov/standards/valuelist/marccarrier.html
- Carrier type for DVD and Blu-ray is "videodisc.".The MARC code is "vd".

340   **Physical Medium**
- Subfield 'b': Dimensions of a DVD disc (4 ¾ in.) may be recorded here.

It's not yet clear how other 340 subfields will be used in RDA for DVDs.

344   **Sound Characteristics**
- RDA 3.16 sound characteristics may be mapped to the new MARC 344.
- For DVDs the following values are appropriate (see Example 1):
    o Subfield 'a': Type of recording (RDA 3.16.2) = digital (for Blu-ray also)
    o Subfield 'b': Recording medium (RDA 3.16.3) = optical (for Blu-ray also)
    o Subfield 'g': Configuration of playback channels (RDA 3.16.8) may be stereo, mono, quadrophonic, or surround.
    o Subfield 'h': Special playback characteristics (RDA 3.16.9), such as Dolby.

346   **Video Characteristics**
- RDA 3.18.3 Broadcast Standard may be recorded in the new MARC 346 subfield 'b' Broadcast standard.
    o DVD and Blu-ray may be HDTV, NTSC, PAL, or SECAM.

347   **Digital File Characteristics**
- For DVD and Blu-Ray, subfields 'a', 'b', and 'e' may be recorded when the information is available.
    o Subfield 'a' File type (RDA 3.19.2) = video file (for DVD and Blu-ray)
    o Subfield 'b' Encoding format (RDA 3.19.3)
        - For DVD, subfield 'b' = DVD video
        - For Blu-ray, subfield 'b' = Blu-ray
        - Subfield 'e' Regional encoding (RDA 3.19.6)

Note: For 344, 346, 347 fields, use $2 rda when terms employed are listed in RDA.

380   **Form of Work**
- RDA 6.3 Form of Work: Form of work is core when needed to differentiate one work from another. It is most often included as part of an authorized access point, but can be optionally recorded as a separate element in the new MARC field 380.
- Example 1 records 380$a as Motion picture.

538   **System Details Note**
- As discussed above, elements recorded in 538 in AACR2 have separate elements in RDA and may also be recorded in the new MARC 34x fields.
- In RDA, the 538 may contain encoding format (3.19.3), regional encoding (3.19.6), special playback characteristics (3.16.9), and broadcast standard (3.18.3).
    o Aspect ratio (RDA 7.19) is mapped to a 500 note in RDA mappings.

Best practices have not been confirmed for use of the 34x field and the 538 note.

546   **Language Note**
- The 546 language note can be used to record the language of the content (RDA 7.12) or to note accessibility content (RDA 7.14).

500   **General Note Used to Record Source of Title**
- In Example 2, a 500 note records the source of the original Italian title.

511   **Participant or Performer Note**
508   **Creation/Production Credits Note (RDA 7.23, 7.24)**
- These notes are pretty much the same in RDA as in AACR2.

500   **General Note Used to Record "Based on" Information**
- A video based on another work has a derivative work relationship to the original work. Optionally, record the relationship (RDA 24.4.3).
- In Example 1, the 500 note is an unstructured description recording the relationship. There is also a 700 name/title entry to express the relationship.

520   **Summary, etc.**
- Summary notes are core only for children's fiction (RDA 7.10.1.3 and the LC-PCC Policy Statement)
- Most video descriptions include a short summary.

521   **Target Audience Note (Example 1)**
- Intended audience is LC core element for resources intended for children, and otherwise optional (RDA 7.7 and LC-PCC Policy Statement).

500   **General Note Used to Record Special Features or Accompanying Material**
- Example 1 provides a note describing special features.
- Example 2 provides a note about the accompanying booklet.

7xx   **Access Points for Creators, Others, Contributors**
- Record the main entities involved in a video work.
  - RDA 19.2 and LC-PCC Policy Statement: Recording the principal creator is RDA core. Recording additional creators is optional.
  - RDA 19.3 and LC-PCC Policy Statement: Recording others associated with a work is core when the name is needed to construct the authorize access point for the work. Otherwise, these relationships are optional.
  - RDA 20.2 and LC-PCC Policy Statement: Contributor is core only for illustrators of children's resources.
- Per PCC guideline number 9, assign relationship designators to all entries using subfield 'e' (PCC 2013, [2]).
  - Creators (Appendix I.2.1): screenwriter
  - Others (Appendix I.2.2): [film] director, film producer, director of photography, production company
  - Contributors (Appendix I.3.1): actor, art director, composer (expression), production designer, interviewee (expression), writer of added text
  - Distributors (Appendix I.4.3): film distributor

700 1_   **$i Motion picture adaptation of (work): $a Haygood, Wil. $t Butler, a witness to history.**
- Appendix J.2.2 Relationship designators for Related Works

MUSICAL SOUND RECORDING (COMPACT DISC—CD)
MUSIC CD—EXAMPLE #1

024 1 _ $a 800413003724
028 0 0 $a CB0037 $b Cold Blue Music
100 1 _ $a Fox, James, $d 1953- $e composer.
245 1 _ ᛫ $a Black water / $c Jim Fox.
264 _ 1 $a Venice, CA : $b Cold Blue Music, $c [2013]
264 _ 4 $c ℗2013
300 _ _ $a 1 audio disc (18 min.) : $b CD audio, stereo ; $c 4 ¾ in.
306 _ _ $a 001805
336 _ _ $a performed music $b prm $2 rdacontent
337 _ _ $a audio $b s $2 rdamedia
338 _ _ $a audio disc $b sd $2 rdacarrier
500 _ _ $a For three pianos.
500 _ _ $a Title from disc label.
511 0 _ $a Bryan Pezzone, pianos.
518 _ _ $o Recorded $d 2006 July $p Architecture, Los Angeles, California.
700 1 _ $a Pezzone, Bryan, $e instrumentalist.

MUSIC CD—EXAMPLE #2

024 3 0 $a 3149024231322
028 0 2 $a 2742313 $b Le Chant du Monde
041 0 _ $d spa $g fre $g spa $g eng
245 0 0 $a Café Domínguez / $c Angel d/Agostino.
264 _ 1 $a [Paris] : $b Le Chant du Monde, $c [2013]
264 _ 2 $b Harmonia Mundi distribution
264 _ 4 $c ℗2013
300 _ _ $a 1 audio disc : $b digital, CD audio, stereo ; $c 4 ¾ in.
336 _ _ $a performed music $b prm $2 rdacontent
337 _ _ $a audio $b s $2 rdamedia
338 _ _ $a audio disc $b sd $2 rdacarrier
340 _ _ $b 4 ¾ in.c
344 _ _ $a digital $b optical $c 1.4 m/s $g stereo $2 rda
347 _ _ $b CD audio $2 rda
546 _ _ $a Sung in Spanish.
500 _ _ $a Title from disc label
511 _ _ $a Orquesta Angel D'Agostina; various singers.
518 _ _ $o Recorded : $d 1941–1955.
500 _ _ $a Insert notes in French, Spanish, and English.
505 0 _ $a Café Domínguez (2:56) – Serpentinas de esperanza (2:54) – Rondando tu esquina (2:53) – A quién le puede importer? (3:12) – Tres esquinas (3:05).
700 1 _ $a Agostino, Angel d', $e performer.

RDA Notes

For more information on music cataloging, see MLA's "Best Practices for Music Cataloging: Using RDA and MARC21." (MLA 2014)

02X   (020, 024, 028) Identifier for the Manifestation/Standard Numbers (RDA 2.15)
- Record all identifiers if feasible (MLA 2014, 28-31).

100   Creator (RDA 19.2)
- Record the composer in the 1xx field. "Composer" is a creator relationship from Appendix I.2.1. (See Example 1.)
- RDA usually considers performers to be contributors. A person or band (corporate body) may be a creator if they composed the work they perform, or have substantially changed it in their performance (MLA 2014, 82). In these cases, they may be entered in the 1xx or 7xx field. Otherwise enter them in 7xx fields. (See Example 2.)

264   Publication Fields
- The copyright © or phonographic copyright ℗ dates can be used to supply a publication date, in square brackets. RDA 2.8.6.6 and LC-PCC Policy Statement 2.8.6.6.
- Record the ℗ date (or © date) in 264 _4 $c. (RDA 2.11).
- Recording Distributor information is not core, but may be recorded separately in a MARC 264 _ 2. See example 2 (RDA 2.9.4).

300   Physical Description
- Subfield 'a' Extent: RDA uses "audio disc" instead of AACR2's "sound disc."
  o RDA 3.4.1.3 and list of carrier types at 3.3.1.3

- Subfield 'b' Other Physical Details: Record other details of sound recordings in 300 $b.
  - RDA 3.19.3: Encoding Format (CD Audio) (and/or in 347 $b)
  - RDA 3.16.2: Type of Recording (digital) (and/or in 344 $a)
  - RDA 3.16.4: Playing Speed (1.4 m/s) (and/or in 344 $c)
  - RDA 3.16.8: Configuration of Playback Channels (stereo/mono/quadrophonic/surround) (and/or in 344 $g)
- Subfield 'c' Dimensions: 4 ¾ in.
  - LC/PCC core for all but serials and online resources (RDA 3.5)

336      $a performed music $b prm $2 rdacontent (RDA 6.9)
337      $a audio $b s $2 rdamedia (RDA 3.2)
338      $a audio disc $b sd $2 rdacarrier (RDA 3.3)
340 $b   Physical Medium, $b Dimensions
- Optionally recorded here. See Example 2 (RDA 3.5).
- MLA shows dimensions in 300 $c for an Audio CD (MLA 2014, 44).

344   Sound Characteristics: Optionally record details of sound characteristics here.
- MARC 344 is new MARC field to accommodate RDA (RDA 3.16).
- Shown in Example 2:
  - Subfield 'a': Type of recording (3.16.2)
  - Subfield 'b': Recording medium (RDA 3.16.3)
    - MLA recommends for sound-track films only (MLA 2014, 40)
  - Subfield 'c': Playing speed (RDA 3.16.4)
    - Not recommended for CDs by MLA (MLA 2014, 44)
  - Subfield 'g': Configuration of playback channels (RDA 3.16.8)
  - Subfield 'h': Special playback characteristics (RDA 3.16.9). MLA recommend recording if feasible (MLA 2014, 42). Information is not included in the examples above.

347   Digital File Characteristics:
MLA recommends recording file type and encoding format for digital audio carriers (MLA 2014, 42).
- MARC 347 is a new MARC field to accommodate RDA (RDA 3.19).
- LC core for cartographic resources. Optional for sound recordings.
- Shown in Example 2:
  - Subfield 'b': Encoding format (RDA 3.19.3)
    - Use a term from the list at 3.19.3.3 (e.g., CD audio)
  - May also record: Subfield 'a': File type (RDA 3.19.2)
    - Use a term from the list at 3.19.2.3 (e.g., audio file).

500   Note: "Title from disc label" (Both examples)
- RDA 2.17.2.3 Title Source: MLA recommends supplying this note for all audio recordings (MLA 2014, 33). Do not follow the option to omit the note when a resource has a single title on the resource itself (LC-PCC PS 2.17.2.3).

511   Participant or Performer Note (RDA 7.23)
- For musical performers, include their medium. See Example 1.

518   Date/Time and Place of an Event Note
- MARC 518 was updated to accommodate these RDA elements.
- RDA 7.11.2 (Place) and RDA 7.11.3 (Date) of capture
- MLA Best Practices recommends including this information for audio and video recordings when it is readily ascertainable (MLA 2014, 73).

700   Added Entry/Personal Name (or 710 Added Entry/Corporate Name for bands)
- *MLA recommendation:* If feasible, give access points for all arrangers, solo performers, conductors, and performing ensembles (MLA 2014, 84).
- Optionally include 7xx entries (name/title or title) for each musical piece (not done in these examples).

AUDIOBOOK (SPOKEN WORD CD)

020 _ _	$a 9780804121521
028 02	$a YA 2106 $b Random House/Listening Library
100 1_	$a Bacigalupi, Paolo, $e author.
245 10	$a Zombie baseball beatdown / $c Paolo Bacigalupi.
250 _ _	$a Unabridged.
264 _1	$a New York : $b Random House/Listening Library, $c [2013]
264 _4	$c ⓟ2013
300 _ _	$a 5 audio discs (6 hr.) : $b digital, CD audio ; $c 4 ¾ in.
306 _ _	$a 060000
336 _ _	$a spoken word $b spw $2 rdacontent
337 _ _	$a audio $b s $2 rdamedia
338 _ _	$a audio disc $b sd $2 rdacarrier
344 _ _	$a digital $b optical $2 rda
511 _ _	$a Read by Sunil Malhotra.
520 _ _	$a While practicing for their next baseball game, threen-year-old friends Rabi, Miguel, and Joe discover that the nefarious activities of the Delbe, Iowa, meat-packing plant have caused cows to turn into zombies.
521 2 _	$a 3–7.
700 1_	$a Malhotra, Sunil, $e narrator.

RDA Notes

300$a	**Extent** • RDA uses "audio disc(s)" instead of sound discs (RDA 3.4.1.3 and list of terms at 3.3.1.3).

300$b	**Other Physical Details**
	• Type of Recording (RDA 3.16.2) may be recorded in 300 $b (and/or in 344 $a).
	  ○ Recording type for a CD is "digital."
	• Encoding Format (RDA Digital File Characteristic, Encoding Format 3.19.3) may be recorded in 300$b.
	  ○ CD encoding format is "CD audio." Terms from list of Audio encoding formats at 3.19.3.3.
	  ○ Encoding format might also be recorded in 347 $b.

336	$a spoken word $b spw $2 rdacontent (RDA 6.9)
337	$a audio $b s $2 rdamedia (RDA 3.2)
338	$a audio disc $b sd $2 rdacarrier (RDA 3.3)

344	**Sound Characteristics**
	• Type of recording (RDA 3.16.2) can be recorded here, in addition to 300 $b.
	  ○ Type of recording for a spoken word CD is "digital."
	• Recording medium (RDA 3.16.3) can be recorded here, in addition to 300 $b. It is not clear whether this will become best practice.
	  ○ Recording medium for a spoken word CD is "optical."

347	**Digital File Characteristics (Field is not included in the example)**
	• File type (RDA 3.19.2) can be recorded in new MARC field 347 $a.
	  ○ File type for a spoken word CD is "audio file."
	• Encoding format (RDA 3.19.3) can be recorded in MARC 300 $b and/or in MARC 347 $b.
	  ○ Encoding format for a spoken word CD is "CD audio."

700	**Added Entry/Personal Name $e Relationship Designator** • Optionally record the narrator as a contributor to the expression (RDA 20.2 and Appendix I.3.1, Relationship Designators for Contributors).

AUDIOBOOK (DOWNLOADABLE)

This is the same title as the Audiobook CD example above, but it is for the downloadable audiobook version of the work. The downloadable record is based on the CD record (see MARC 588 and 776).

100 1_ $a Bacigalupi, Paolo, $e author.
245 10 $a Zombie baseball beatdown / $c by National Book Award finalist Paolo Bacigalupi.
250 _ _ $a Unabridged.
264 _1 $a New York : $b Random House/Listening Library, $c [2013]
300 _ _ $a 1 online resource (1 audio file)
306 _ _ $a 060000
336 _ _ $a spoken word $b spw $2 rdacontent
337 _ _ $a computer $b s $2 rdamedia
338 _ _ $a online resource $b sd $2 rdacarrier
344 _ _ $a digital $2 rda
347 _ _ $a audio file $2 rda
511 _ _ $a Read by Sunil Malhotra.
520 _ _ $a While practicing for their next baseball game, thirteen-year-old friends Rabi, Miguel, and Joe discover that the nefarious activities of the Delbe, Iowa, meat-packing plant have caused cows to turn into zombies.
538 _ _ $a Requires Acoustik audio app.
588 _ _ $a Description based on original audiobook record.
521 2_ $a 3–7.
700 1_ $a Malhotra, Sunil, $e narrator.
776 08 $i Electronic reproduction of (manifestation) : $a Bacigalupi, Paolo. $t Zombie baseball beatdown $d New York, New York : Listening Library, [2013] $w (OCoLC) 848826009

RDA Notes

300    $a Extent (RDA 3.4.1.3 and 3.3.1.3)
- Specify type and number of units. "1 online resource" (RDA 3.4.1.3 and 3.3.1.3).
- RDA 3.4.1.7.5—Record subunits using a term from 3.19.2.3 "(1 audio file)"

336    $a spoken word (RDA 6.9)
337    $a computer (RDA 3.2)
338    $a online resource (RDA 3.3)
344   Sound Characteristics
- RDA 3.16.2, Sound Characteristic/Type of Recording:
  o For a downloadable audiobook the type of recording is "digital."

347   Digital File Characteristics
- Record the File Type (RDA 3.19.2.3)—"audio file."

538   System Details Note
- RDA 3.20, Equipment or System Requirements

588   Source of Description Note (RDA 2.17.13)
- Provide a source of description note when the record is based on a record for the same title in a different format. Format the note as:
  o "Description based on [physical format] version record" (PCC "Provider-Neutral E-Resource 2012, 17)
- Use in combination with a 776 field.

776   Additional Physical Form
  • Use MARC 776 to express the relationship between the audiobook and the
    e-audio expressions (RDA 27.1).
  • Give a structured description (subfields $a, $b) and provide identifiers in
    subfield 'w'.
856   Electronic Location and Access (4.6.1.3)
  • This field is not included in the example record. Libraries usually include a
    URL for their institution in their local catalog record.

E-BOOK

020 _ _ $a 9781134019632 (electronic bk.)
020 _ _ $z 9780415479998 (print)
040 _ _ $a AAA $b eng $e rda $e pn
100 1 _ $a Maton, Karl.
245 10 $a Knowledge and knowers : $b towards a realist sociology of education / $c
           Karl Maton.
264 _ 1 $a Milton Park, Abingdon, Oxon : $b Routledge ,$c 2014.
300 _ _ $a 1 online resource (xii, 244 pages)
336 _ _ $a text $b txt $2 rdacontent
337 _ _ $a computer $b c $2 rdamedia
338 _ _ $a online resource $b cr $2 rdacarrier
504 _ _ $a Includes bibliographical references and index.
588 _ _ $a Description based on print version record.
776 08 $i Print version: $a Maton, Karl. $t Knowledge and knowers $z 9780415479998
           $w (DLC) 2013008156 $w (OCoLC)842337220
856 40 $3 EBSCOhost $u http://search.ebscohost.com/login.
           aspx?direct=true&scope=site&db=nlebk&db=nlabk&AN=639634

RDA Notes

The example follows PCC's Provider-Neutral E-Resource: MARC Record Guide: P-N/RDA
version.
020   ISBN (RDA 2.15, Core)
  • Subfield $a: Record the e-book ISBN. Record multiple e-book ISBNs in sepa-
    rate 020$a fields. (Qualifier in $q after 9/2013.)
  • Subfield $z: Record other ISBNs (e.g., for print editions).

040
  • $e pn: Add a second subfield 'e' with "pn" to specify Provider Neutral.
264 _1   Publication Statement
  • When following the Provider Neutral guidelines, information will come
    from the original tangible source record rather than the electronic version.
    This practice is counter to RDA if the e-book is considered a reproduction.
    RDA would provide the reproduction information here (RDA 2.8.1.3, PCC
    "Provider-Neutral E-Resource" 2012, 9).
300   Physical Description
  • Subfield $a Extent, RDA 3.4:
    o "1 online resource" (xii, 244 pages)
    o Subunits (e.g., pages) recommended, but optional
  • Subfield $b Other Physical Characteristics
    o May note presence of illustrative (RDA 7.15) or other content (optional).

- Subfield $c Dimensions: RDA 3.5:
  - Do not include dimensions for online resources (PCC "Provider-Neutral E-Resource" 2012, 12).
336   **$a text $b txt $2 rdacontent (RDA 6.9)**
- Additional content types may be appropriate (e.g., for still images).
337   **$a computer $b c $2 rdamedia (RDA 3.2)**
338   **$a online resource $b cr $2 rdacarrier (RDA 3.3)**
347   **Digital File Characteristics (RDA 3.19)**
- Optional for e-books (core for cartographic resources, LC-PCC PS)
- 347 $a: File type "text file" for e-books if used (RDA 3.19.2.3)
- Do not include file size (RDA 3.19.4) for Provider Neutral records (PCC "Provider-Neutral E-Resource" 2012, 13).
588   **Source of Description (RDA 2.17.13)**
- Provider Neutral guidelines (p. 17) specify that if the electronic version is based on a physical version, the 588 note should be formatted as:
  - "Description based on [physical format] version record"
- Use in combination with a 776 field.
776   **Additional Physical Form**
- RDA 27.1: Give a structured description (subfields $a, $b) and provide identifiers in subfield 'w'.
856   **Electronic Location and Access (4.6.1.3)**
- Include general URLs for the resource here. Use subfield 'u.'
- Add the local URL for your institution to your local record.

VIDEO GAME

245 00   **$a Mario & Sonic at the Olympic winter games. $p Sochi 2014.**
246 3_   **$a Mario and Sonic at the Olympic winter games. $p Sochi 2014**
246 1_   **$i Title from container spine: $a Mario & Sonic at the Sochi 2014 Olympic winter games**
264 _1   **$a Redmond, WA : $b Nintendo of America, Inc., $c [2013?]**
264 _4   **$c ©2013.**
300 _ _   **$a 1 computer disc : $b sound, color ; $c 4 ¾ in.**
336 _ _   **$a two-dimensional moving image $b tdi $2 rdacontent**
337 _ _   **$a computer $b c $2 rdamedia**
338 _ _   **$a computer disc $b cd $2 rdacarrier**
520 _ _   **$a Legendary rivals face off in the ultimate winter competition.**
521 _ _   **$a E, Everyone.**
538 _ _   **$a System requirements: Nintendo Wii U; Wii remotes for multiplayer.**
546 _ _   **$a Game, container, and booklet content in English, French, and Spanish.**
710 2_   **$a Nintendo of America, Inc., $e production company.**

RDA Notes

300   **$a Extent (RDA 3.4.1.3 and 3.3.1.3)**
- "1 computer disc"
300   **$b Other Physical Characteristics**
- RDA 7.18 Color content
- RDA 7.17 Sound content
336   **$a two dimensional moving image $b tdi $2 rdacontent (RDA 6.9)**
- Might use second content type "computer program"
337   **$a computer $b c $2 rdamedia (RDA 3.2)**

338        $a computer disc $b cd $2 rdacarrier (RDA 3.3)
380   Form of Work
           • RDA 6.3, Form of Work
           • Optionally record the term "Video game" as the form of work in MARC
             380.
710   Added Entry/Corporate Name
           • Production Company = Other person, family, corporate body associated with
             a work relationship (RDA 19.3 and Appendix I.2.2)

ONLINE INTEGRATING RESOURCE

245 00 $a Daily mail historical archive 1896–2004.
264 _1 $a [Michigan] : $b Gale Cengage Learning, $c [2013?]–
300 _ _ $a 1 online resource
336 _ _ $a text $2 rdacontent
336 _ _ $a still image $2 rdacontent
337 _ _ $a computer $2 rdamedia
338 _ _ $a online resource $2 rdacarrier
362 1_ $a Coverage begins with no. 1 (May 4, 1896).
588 _ _ $a Description based on version viewed August 30, 2013; title from home
           screen.
856 40 $a Online archive $u http://infotrac.galegroup.com/web/44444?db=XXXX

RDA Notes

264 _1   Give place and publisher name. when available. Provide a date of first iteration if
           possible. (RDA 2.8.6.5)

300        $a Specify extent as "1 online resource" (RDA 3.4.1.3, see examples)
           $b Other Physical Characteristics are optional
           $c Dimensions: Do not record dimensions for online resources (PCC "Provid-
           er-Neutral E-Resources 2012, 12)

336        $a text
336        $a still image
           Specify at least one content type. Additional content types are optional, but can
           be recorded. (RDA 6.9)
337        $a computer (RDA 3. 2)
338        $a online resource (RDA 3.3)

362   If available, provide a date for the beginning of coverage (original iteration)
           (RDA 2.6)

588   Date of viewing of an online resource (RDA 2.17.13.5)
           • Sometimes provided in a 500 note

856   Electronic Location and Access (RDA 4.6.1.3)
           • Uniform Resource Locator

ONLINE SERIAL (E-JOURNAL)

```
022 0_   $a 2333-6285 $2 1
040 _ _  $aLLL $b eng $e rda $c LLL
222 _0   $a Posit
245 00   $a Posit : $b a journal of literature and art.
264 _1   $a [New York, NY] : $b [Susan Lewis], $c [2013-]
310 _ _  $a Three times a year
336 _ _  $a text $b txt $2 rdacontent
337 _ _  $a computer $b˙c $2 rdamedia
338 _ _  $a online resource $b cr $2 rdacarrier
362 1_   $a Began with: 1.
588_ _   $a Description based on: 1; title from banner (journal homepage, viewed Feb. 5,
         2014).
588 _ _  $a Latest issue consulted: 1 (viewed Feb. 5, 2014).
856 40   $u http://positjournal.com
```

RDA Notes

```
336   $a text $b txt $2 rdacontent (RDA 6.9)
337   $a computer $b c $2 rdamedia (RDA 3.2)
338   $a online resource $b cr $2 rdacarrier (RDA 3.3)
588   Source of Description Note
```
- RDA 2.17.13 Note on issue, part, or iteration used as the basis for identification of the resource
- RDA 2.17.13.3.1: Latest issue consulted note

STREAMING AUDIO (MUSIC)

```
100 1_   $a Oberon, Edward, $e composer, $e performer.
245 10   $a Reset E.P. / $c Edward Oberon, Need for Mirrors.
264 _ 1  $a [New Zealand] : $b V Recordings, $c [2013]
300 _ _  $a 1 online resource (4 audio files)
336 _ _  $a performed music $2 rdacontent
337 _ _  $a computer $2 rdamedia
338 _ _  $a online resource $2 rdacarrier
344 _ _  $a digital $2 rda
347 _ _  $a audio file $b FLAC
588 _ _  $a Description based on online resource; title from file host. $5 XX
710 2_   $a Need for Mirrors (Musical group), $e performer.
856 42   $3 File host $u http://www.beatport.com/release/reset-ep/1110042
856 4_   $u http://musicdeliver.natlib/contentaggregator/getIEs?system=ilsdb&id=
         1617416 $y Archived copy available within Library only $x Lib Access Right =
         200
```

RDA Notes

```
300$a   Extent
```
- RDA 3.4: Record the number and type of unit. Record type and number of subunits (term from 3.19.2.3 File Type).
```
336   $a performed music $2 rdacontent (RDA 6.9)
337   $a computer $2 rdamedia (RDA 3.2)
338   $a online resource $2 rdacarrier (RDA 3.3)
```

344   Sound Characteristics
         • RDA 3.16.2 Type of Recording "digital"
347   Digital File Characteristics
         • Subfield 'a': RDA 3.19.2 File Type "audio file"
         • Subfield 'b': RDA 3.19.3 Encoding Format

STREAMING VIDEO

245 02 $a A Master United States Catalog of Subgrade Soil-Water Characteristic Curve
         Default Input Values for the MEPDG.
264 _ 1 $a Washington, D.C. : $b Transportation Research Board, $c 2010.
300 _ _ $a 1 online resource (84 min.) : $b digital, sound, color
336 _ _ $a two-dimensional moving image $b tdi $2 rdacontent
337 _ _ $a computer $b c $2 rdamedia
337 _ _ $a video $b v $2 rdamedia
338 _ _ $a online resource $b cr $2 rdacarrier
511 0_ $a Panelist: Claudia Zapata, Arizona State University. Moderated by: Matthew
         Witczak, Arizona State University.
508 _ _ $a Produced by the Transportation Research Board of the National Academies.
520 _ _ $a On Wednesday, March 17, 2010, TRB conducted a web briefing or "webi-
         nar" that explored TRB's National Cooperative Highway Research Program
         Project 9-23A
700 1_ $a Zapata, Claudia E. $q (Claudia Elena), $e speaker.
700 1_ $a Witczak, Matthew W., $e moderator.
710 2_ $a National Research Council (U.S.). $b Transportation Research Board, $e
         producer.
856 40 $u http://www.lib. . . . $y View resource online (XXX University only)

RDA Notes

336      $a two-dimensional moving image $b tdi $2 rdacontent (RDA 6.9)
337      $a computer $b c $2 rdamedia (RDA 3.2)
337      $a video $2 rdamedia
         • For streaming video, some libraries record a second media type for "video."
338      $a online resource $b cr $2 rdacarrier (RDA 3.3)
347      $a Digital File Characteristics/File Type
         • RDA 3.19.2.3 Recording File Type: Some libraries record file type "video
         file" in the MARC 347 subfield 'a'.

Bibliography and Works Cited

Arakawa, Steven. "RDA Basics: Applying Resource Description and Access in a MARC/ISBD Environment." Presented at NELA Annual, 2012. http://netsl.files.wordpress.com/2012/10/rdabasicsnela2012.pdf (cited July 20, 2014).

Ehlert, Mark K. "RDA Notes." *Minitex Digitization, Cataloging & Metadata Mailing* March/April 2014: 3–10. http://minitex.umn.edu/Communications/Mailing/2014/03March.pdf (cited July 10, 2014).

El-Sherbini, Magda. *RDA: Strategies for Implementation.* Chicago: ALA Editions, 2013.

"Entity Relationship Diagram: Manifestation." *In* RDA Toolkit: RDA Background. http://www.rdatoolkit.org/backgroundfiles/Manifestation_6_1_09-1.pdf (cited February 20, 2014).

Glennan, Kathy. "RDA: Revising, Developing, and Assessing." An ALA ALCTS webinar presented on February 19, 2014. Recording available at http://www.ala.org/alcts/confevents/upcoming/webinar/021914 (cited March 31, 2014).

IFLA (International Federation of Library Associations and Institutions) Study Group on the Functional Requirements for Bibliographic Records. *Functional Requirements for Bibliographic Records: Final Report.* 1998. http://www.ifla.org/files/assets/cataloguing/frbr/frbr_2008.pdf (cited July 10, 2014).

IFLA (International Federation of Library Associations and Institutions) Study Group on the Functional Requirements for Bibliographic Records. Working Group on Functional Requirements and Numbering of Authority Records. *Functional Requirement for Authority Data.* Amended and corrected July 2013. http://www.ifla.org/files/assets/cataloguing/frad/frad_2013.pdf (cited July 10, 2014).

IFLA (International Federation of Library Associations and Institutions) Study Group on the Functional Requirements for Bibliographic Records. IME-ICC (IFLA Meetings of Experts on an International Cataloguing Code). *Statement of International Cataloguing Principles.* 2009. http://www.ifla.org/files/assets/cataloguing/icp/icp_2009-en.pdf (cited February 20, 2014).

Jin, Qiang. *Demystifying FRAD: Functional Requirements for Authority Data.* Santa Barbara, California: Libraries Unlimited, 2012.

JSC (Joint Steering Committee for Development of RDA). "A Brief History of AACR2." http://www.rda-jsc.org/history.html (cited July 10, 2014).

JSC (Joint Steering Committee for Development of RDA). "FRBR-RDA Mapping." Revised 2009. Working Documents, RDA Document Series. http://www.rda-jsc .org/docs/5rda-frbrrdamappingrev.pdf (cited July 10, 2014).

JSC (Joint Steering Committee for Development of RDA). "Outcomes of the Meeting of the Joint Steering Committee Held in Chicago, U.S.A., 24–28 April, 2005." Historic Documents. http://www.rda-jsc.org/0504out.html (cited July 10, 2014).

JSC (Joint Steering Committee for Development of RDA). "Outcomes of the Meeting of the Joint Steering Committee Held in Chicago, U.S.A., 15–20 October 2007." Historic Documents. http://www.rda-jsc.org/0710out.html (cited July 10, 2014).

JSC (Joint Steering Committee for Development of RDA). "Strategic Plan for RDA 2005–2009." http://www.rda-jsc.org/stratplan.html (cited July 10, 2014).

JSC (Joint Steering Committee for Development of RDA). "RDA/ONIX Framework for Resource Categorization." 2006. Working Documents, Chair Documents Series. http://www.rda-jsc.org/docs/5chair10.pdf, available at http://www.rda -jsc.org/working2.html#chair-10 (cited July 11, 2014).

Library of Congress. "Library of Congress Announces Its Long-Range RDA Training Plan (Updated March 2, 2012)." http://www.loc.gov/catdir/cpso/news_rda_ implementation_date.html (cited July 10, 2014).

Library of Congress. "Library of Congress (LC) RDA Training Materials." http:// www.loc.gov/catworkshop/RDA%20training%20materials/LC%20RDA%20 Training/LC%20RDA%20course%20table.html (cited July 11, 2014).

Library of Congress. "RDA: Module 1—Introduction to RDA; Identifying Manifestations and Items [Manual]" 2012. http://www.loc.gov/catworkshop/RDA%20 training%20materials/LC%20RDA%20Training/Module1IntroManifestItems- Sept12.doc (cited July 10, 2014).

Library of Congress. "RDA: Module 2—Describing Carriers and Identifying Works [Manual]" 2012. http://www.loc.gov/catworkshop/RDA%20training%20ma terials/LC%20RDA%20Training/Module2CarriersAndWorksSept12.doc (cited July 11, 2014).

Library of Congress. "RDA Module 3 – Identifying Expressions and Describing Content [Manual]" 2012. http://www.loc.gov/catworkshop/RDA%20training%20 materials/LC%20RDA%20Training/Module3ExpressionsAndContentSept12. doc (cited July 20, 2014).

Library of Congress. "RDA: Module 4 – Relationships in RDA [Manual]" Revised December 2012. http://www.loc.gov/catworkshop/RDA%20training%20ma terials/LC%20RDA%20Training/Module%204_Relationships.doc (cited July 10, 2014).

Library of Congress Network Development and MARC Standards Office. "MARC Code List for Languages." 2007 edition. http://www.loc.gov/marc/languages/ (cited July 11, 2014).

Library of Congress Network Development and MARC Standards Office. "Term and Code List for RDA Carrier Types." http://www.loc.gov/standards/valuelist/rdacarrier.html (cited July 9, 2014).

Library of Congress Network Development and MARC Standards Office. "Term and Code List for RDA Content Types." http://www.loc.gov/standards/valuelist/rdacontent.html (cited July 9, 2014).

Library of Congress Network Development and MARC Standards Office. "Term and Code List for RDA Media Types." http://www.loc.gov/standards/valuelist/rdamedia.html (cited July 9, 2014).

Library of Congress Working Group on the Future of Bibliographic Control. "On the Record." Library of Congress, 2008. http://www.loc.gov/bibliographic-future/news/lcwg-ontherecord-jan08-final.pdf (cited July 10, 2014)

Marcum, Deanna B. "Joint Statement of the Library of Congress, the National Library of Medicine, and the National Agricultural Library on Resource Description and Access." May 2008. http://www.loc.gov/bibliographic-future/news/RDA_Letter_050108.pdf (cited July 10, 2014).

Maurer, Margaret. "RDA Travelogue—Choose Your Own Adventures Handout." 2013. http://www.personal.kent.edu/~mbmaurer/documents/Decisions tobemade_001.pdf, available at http://www.personal.kent.edu/~mbmaurer/RDA TravelogueOCLC.html (cited March 28, 2014).

Maurer, Margaret, and Erin Stalberg. "RDA Implementation Experiences: An OCLC Webinar." Presented by OCLC on October 16, 2013. Recording available at https://www.oclc.org/events/2013/rdawebinar101613.en.html (cited March 28, 2014).

MLA (Music Library Association) RDA Music Implementation Task Force. "Best Practices for Music Cataloging: Using RDA and MARC21, Version 1.0.1." April 2014. http://bcc.musiclibraryassoc.org/BCC-Historical/BCC2014/RDA%20Best%20Practices%20for%20Music%20Cataloging_v101.pdf (cited July 10, 2014).

NCSU (North Carolina State University) Libraries Intranet. "RDA." https://staff.lib.ncsu.edu/confluence/display/MNC/RDA (cite July 20, 2014).

OCLC. "OCLC RDA Policy Statement." March 31, 2013. http://oclc.org/rda/new-policy.en.html (cited July 10, 2014).

Oliver, Chris. Introducing RDA: A Guide to the Basics. Chicago: American Library Association, 2010.

PCC-LC (Program for Cooperative Cataloging and Library of Congress). "Summary of Programmatic Changes to the LC/NACO Authority File: What LC-PCC RDA Catalogers Need to Know." July, 30, 2012. http://www.loc.gov/aba/rda/pdf/lcnaf_rdaphase.pdf (cited July 10, 2014).

PCC (Program for Cooperative Cataloging). "RDA Authorities Phase 3 Task Group [Report]," March 18, 2014. http://www.loc.gov/aba/pcc/rda/RDA%20Task%20groups%20and%20charges/RDA-Auth-Phase3-TG.docx, available at http://www.loc.gov/aba/pcc/rda/RDA%20Task%20Groups.html (cited July 10, 2014).

PCC (Program for Cooperative Cataloging). "Post-Implementation Hybrid Bibliographic Records Guidelines Task Group Report." 2012, revised 2013. http://

www.loc.gov/aba/pcc/rda/RDA Task groups and charges/PCC-Hybrid-Bib-Rec-Guidelines-TG-Report.docx (cited July 10, 2014).

PCC (Program for Cooperative Cataloging). "PCC Update Midwinter 2014." February 18, 2014. http://www.loc.gov/aba/pcc/PCC-Update-ALA-MW2014.pdf (cited July 10, 2014).

PCC (Program for Cooperative Cataloging). "PCC Guidelines for the Application of Relationship Designators in Bibliographic Records." 2013. http://www.loc.gov/aba/pcc/rda/PCC RDA guidelines/Relat-Desig-Guidelines.docx, available at http://www.loc.gov/aba/pcc/rda/PCC%20RDA%20guidelines/Post-RDA-Implementation-Guidelines.html (cited July 11, 2014).

PCC (Program for Cooperative Cataloging). "Provider-Neutral E-Resource: MARC Record Guide: P-N/RDA version." 2012, revised January 1, 2013. http://www.loc.gov/aba/pcc/scs/documents/PN-RDA-Combined.docx, available at http://www.loc.gov/aba/pcc/scs/documents/PCC-PN-guidelines.html (cited July 11, 2014).

PCC/SCT (Standing Committee on Training) Records Task Group. "RDA Record Examples." http://www.loc.gov/catworkshop/RDA%20training%20materials/SCT%20RDA%20Records%20TG/index.html (cited July 20, 2014).

PCC/SCT (Standing Committee on Training) RDA Training Materials Task Group. "Recommended Materials." http://www.loc.gov/catworkshop/RDA%20training%20materials/SCT%20RDA%20Training%20Materials%20TG/ (cited July 20, 2014).

RDA to MARC Bibliographic Mapping. Chicago: American Library Association; Ottawa: Canadian Library Association; London: Chartered Institute of Library and Information Professionals (CILIP), 2010. http://access.rdatoolkit.org [Tools Tab, RDA Mappings] (cited July 11, 2014).

RDA Toolkit. Chicago: American Library Association; Ottawa: Canadian Library Association; London: Chartered Institute of Library and Information Professionals (CILIP), 2010. http://www.rdatoolkit.org/ (cited July15, 2014).

Schiff, Adam. "Changes from AACR2 to RDA: A Comparison of Examples Part 1: Description. 2012. http://faculty.washington.edu/aschiff/UW2012Presentation-Part1-Notes.pdf (cited July 20, 2104).

Schiff, Adam. "Changes from AACR2 to RDA: A Comparison of Examples Part 2: Access Points. 2012. http://faculty.washington.edu/aschiff/UW2012Presentation-Part2-Notes.pdf (cited July 20, 2014).

Stanford University Libraries. Metadata Department. "Videos—Cataloging (RDA). http://lib.stanford.edu/metadata-department/clone-video-cataloging-guidelines. Also available from PCC/SCT RDA Training Materials Task Group at http://www.loc.gov/catworkshop/RDA%20training%20materials/SCT%20RDA%20Training%20Materials%20TG/ (cited July 20, 3014).

Tillett, Barbara. "AACR3: Resource Description and Access." Presented at ALA Annual, Orlando, 2004. http://www.ala.org/alcts/sites/ala.org.alcts/files/content/events/pastala/annual/04/tillettch12.pdf (cited July 10, 2014).

U.S. RDA Test Coordinating Committee. "Report and Recommendations of the U.S. RDA Test Coordinating Committee." 2011. http://www.loc.gov/bibliographic -future/rda/source/rdatesting-finalreport-20june2011.pdf (cited July 10, 2014).

U.S. RDA Test Coordinating Committee. "Final U.S. RDA Implementation Update from the U.S. RDA Test Coordinating Committee." 2013. http://www.loc.gov/ aba/rda/pdf/RDA_updates_04jan13.pdf (cited July 10, 2014).

Index

About the Author

AMY HART has been a technical services/systems librarian for more than 20 years, most recently serving as head of bibliographic services at Minuteman Library Network in Natick, MA. Her published work includes ABC-CLIO's *The RDA Primer: A Guide for the Occasional Cataloger* as well as several articles in *Library Media Connection,* for which she also serves as a reviewer. She earned her degree in library and information studies at University College Dublin, Ireland.